So, you're <u>not</u> a perfect parent?

Don't worry. It's a well-known fact that most parents aren't infallible. As surprising as it might seem, despite all the best resources on child raising available to them, parents still make mistakes occasionally! The good news is that we can always learn from our mistakes. And Bill Butterworth has learned an awful lot! In **My Kids Are My Best Teachers,** he offers you realistic wisdom he learned the hard way — through trial and error. With warmth, sincerity, and a touch of humor, he presents "The ABC's of Parenting" — sort of a practical primer for less-than-perfect parents. As you read these alphabetized vignettes of family situations, you'll discover some pretty insightful, down-to-earth advice on a variety of topics: God . . . love . . . relationships . . . discipline . . . fun . . . self-control . . . time . . . and all the really important things in life. Each chapter concludes with a short project designed to get you off to a good start in implementing these lessons in your own family. As a parent, you'll find out sooner or later when you've done right and when you've goofed up. In **My Kids Are My Best Teachers,** you're sure to learn a thing or two the easy way.

BY Bill Butterworth

Peanut Butter Families Stick Together
My Kids Are My Best Teachers—The ABCs of Parenting

My Kids Are My Best Teachers: The ABCs of Parenting

Bill Butterworth

Fleming H. Revell Company
Old Tappan, New Jersey

Scripture quotations in this book are taken from the New American Standard Bible, © The Lockman Foundation 1960, 1962, 1963, 1968, 1971, 1972, 1973, 1975, 1977. Used by permission.

Hand printing by Joy Butterworth.

Library of Congress Cataloging-in-Publication Data

Butterworth, Bill.
My kids are my best teachers—the ABCs of parenting.

1. Parenting. 2. Parenting—Religious aspects—Christianity. I. Title.
HQ755.8.B87 1986 649′.1 85-25795
ISBN 0-8007-5210-4

Published by Fleming H. Revell Company
Old Tappan, New Jersey 07675

Printed in the United States of America

This is a book about the fine faculty God has given me as a student of living. Therefore, it is lovingly and gratefully dedicated to my terrific tribe of teachers. Every one of them. For they each teach.

—*To Joy*

Thank you for teaching me the priority of love and laughter. I love you.

—*To Jesse*

Thank you for teaching me the value of creativity and confidence. I love you.

—*To Jeffrey*

Thank you for teaching me the wisdom in sensitivity and mystery. I love you.

—*To John*

Thank you for teaching me the importance of enthusiasm and straightforwardness. I love you.

—*To Joseph*

Thank you for teaching me the need for mellowness and innocence. I love you.

—*And to Rhonda*

Thank you for being the Dean of my faculty, my fellow student, and most of all, my Best Friend, both in and out of class. I love you.

[illegible]

To Dad

Thank you for teaching me the meaning of [illegible] love. I love you.

To [illegible]

Thank you for [illegible] confidence. I love you.

To [illegible]

Thank you for teaching me [illegible] I love you.

To [illegible]

Thank you for [illegible] I love you.

To [illegible]

Thank you for teaching me the meaning of [illegible] I love you.

To [illegible]

Thank you for [illegible] love [illegible] and [illegible] I love you.

CONTENTS

I have the audacity to make mistakes as a parent.

I know that's hard to believe, because I'm a parent who also happens to be a Christian. Christian parents aren't supposed to make mistakes . . . they leave mistakes to their non-Christian neighbors. After all, part of my witness to my world is my perfect home.

Some of you can't believe that a Christian parent could occasionally drop the ball. One look at the multitude of resources available and it boggles the mind to think there's some idiot out there messing up!

Well, it's not because I've avoided those resources. Check out this list of my accomplishments:

- I've "dared to discipline."
  I was double-dared back.
- I've tried to "make my child mind without losing mine."
  I lost it.
- I tried "hide or seek."
  The kids said, "Hide."
- I tried to typify *What Kids Need Most in a Dad.*
  They said, "Anything but Boy George."
- I viewed my children as "wet cement."
  They dried.
- I read *Letters to Philip* and *Letters to Karen* so many times I'm now corresponding with them myself.
- I "instituted basic youth conflicts."
  They joined right in.
- I "focused on my family."
  It's still blurry.

- I've "improved my serve,"
  "strengthened my grip,"
  "dropped my guard,"
  "seasoned my life,"
  "struck my original match,"
  and "handed my kids another
  brick."

The kids said, "No fair, you work for him!
You probably didn't even *pay* for the books!"

Now don't take me wrong. I have nothing but love and respect for all these folks. These are all quality people with good solid stuff. So I'm not knocking them. I must confess, I did get things working for me . . . at times.

But this is a book about the other times. You know, the times you try, but fail, or the times you don't try and succeed.

So, with all due respect to the great ones on the preceding list, if you've had some rough days recently with the kids, this book is for you.

I learn a lot about parenting through trial and error. Mostly error. But the point is, I *do learn.* This book is a catalog of some of my attempts to do what's expected of a dad. It has the thrill of victory, the agony of defeat, and hopefully, the markings of a realistic family in the process of helping each other along the way.

You'll notice the emphasis on ABCs. This approach is developed for a specific reason. When parents are making mistakes, frustrated, or fighting to cope, they don't need the advanced seminar. They need the basics.

It's like Vince Lombardi's old line when his Green Bay Packers were struggling, "Gentlemen, this is a football!" I have a feeling if Lombardi were still living and he came over to our house one evening for a social visit, before the night was through he would pick up one of my children and say to me, "Butterworth, this is a kid!"

It helps to get a handle on the basics.

This is by no means the last word on parenting. There are many many more ABCs that could be developed, but these are the ones that have greatest relevance to my life right now. And since I meet so many people who are in the same place I am right now, I'd venture to say it will have great relevance to *your* life right now.

The chapters are short, because these lessons find their way out of my children's lives. It's been my observation that lessons from little ones are like lightning: quick and sometimes painful. There are no long-winded profs in the mini-kid mold.

It's kind of a chronicle of human nature at the Butterworth house. It's lessons of life learned in love. All the bases are covered: God, life, love, relationships, discipline, reality, self-control, time, and what's really important in our world. Some will make you laugh. Some will make you misty-eyed. All make memories. You'll see yourself and your kids on quite a few pages.

I'd love for you to walk through these ABCs with me. In order to encourage you to work through this stuff, there's a short project at the end of each lesson. These projects are under the heading "Making It Stick." Some are fun, some will create a little tension, some you talk through, some you write, some you act. They all lead to change—for the better!

It's time for school to begin. So join me in jamming that adult body into a second grader's desk. Stay with me in this book, okay? If you do, I promise, I'll give you an extra fifteen minutes at recess.

My Kids Are My Best Teachers: The ABCs of Parenting

All Over a Dumb Old Football

There's something magical about a birthday when you're a kid.

Remember the feeling? You gain a whole year on all your friends in just one day. They stay four . . . or seven . . . or three, but you go to bed as a five-year-old and wake up the next morning a big boy of six.

It's a special day and should be carefully planned.

Those sentiments came through loud and clear from my son Jesse when he went from formerly five, to solidly six. He wanted a birthday party at a certain place, with certain friends, a certain menu, a certain type of birthday cake, and certainly gifts.

Jesse's not the type of kid to spout off a list of gifts a mile long. True, he does have every aisle at TOYS "Я" US committed to memory, but he is very thoughtful about his choices for potential presents.

So when I asked him what he wanted for his birthday, I expected a well-planned reply. I was ready for suggestions like (1) a baseball glove [aisle 6 below the batting helmets], (2) Stomper 4 × 4 race cars [aisle 17 next to the G.I. Joe remote-controlled tanks], or (3) Parcheesi Board Game [games are alphabetical in aisle 1 . . . it's between Pac Man and Pay Day].

However, I didn't get any of those answers. I was given a lesson in love instead.

"Dad, I'd like a ball to play with for my birthday," was Jesse's carefully planned reply.

"Great," I responded, "What kind of ball do you want?"

"I think I'd like either a football or a soccer ball."

"Okay," I agreed, but pressed him further. "Which would you like more, a football or a soccer ball?"

"Welllll . . . " he mused slowly.

I should have known, by his pause, that it was coming.

"Wellll . . . if you had some time to play ball with me this next year, I'd really like a football for you and me to throw around in the backyard. But if you're gonna be real busy again this year, maybe you just better get me a soccer ball, because I can play soccer with the rest of the kids in the neighborhood."

He paused again. The silence was deafening.

"Uhhh . . . well . . . okay, buddy . . . I will . . . uhhh . . . I will make a choice and uh . . . surprise you on your birthday.

"Great, Daddy . . . I love you. . . ."

I grabbed my wife and went into another room to relay the conversation that had just transpired. It was as I was retelling the story that my son's real message came through—

He wasn't longing for gifts.

He was longing for the *giver*.

You know, as Christians, we can get so wrapped up in the externals of Christianity—the actions, the mechanics, the settings, the trappings, the gifts—that we forget about the Giver.

It took an almost-six-year-old to remind me that relationships are more important than things. It's true in our family. It's true in God's family.

By the way, the oddest thing occurred on my son's sixth birthday. It's a moment we'll never forget—

A grown man and a little boy embracing and sobbing tears of joy.

All over a dumb old football.

Aa

Appreciate the _giver_ as well as the gift.

Making It Stick

Gifts are important to children, but GIVERS are important, too. Think back to the last gift-giving occasion at your house. It may be Christmas or a birthday or a graduation or something unique to your family. How much attention was focused on the gifts themselves? How much attention was focused on appreciating the givers? This is an important concept for a child to grasp. I want my kids to appreciate those who give the gifts just as much as the gift proper.

Here's a couple of hints from our house. First, I find our kids easily and eagerly appreciate us when we're *sensitive* to their requests. There were several soccer balls on the block, but it was a football that was the real prize in our neighborhood. It's subtle, but as my wife tells me when we're in the toy store, "We're shopping for the kids, not for you!"

Another way to appreciate the giver is by seeing the giver in the gift. The football meant Jesse was getting ME for his birthday. I like homemade gifts that have the unmistakable mark of the individual giver. On each child's birthday, I write a little poem—all about that child in my own style. It's a special moment.

So, come on, fellow givers, let's stand up and be counted. Don't get tossed aside with the ribbons and wrappings!

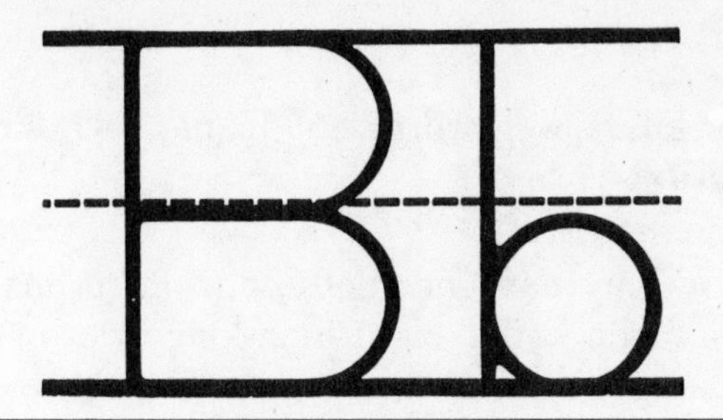

Beauty and Simplicity

There is beauty in simplicity. And there is simplicity in beauty.

Occasionally, when I can block out my world of complexity, I love to watch my kids play. It is beautiful. It is simple. Joy has her little dolly. Dolly doesn't walk, talk, wet, skate, crawl, sit up, fetch, cry, eat, wave, sing, or do windows.

But Joy loves her.

Because with that simple little cloth doll, Joy can transform herself into her idol . . . her Mama. She can put the dolly in a cardboard shoe box and pretend it's a crib. She can hold that little baby and give her the love and physical contact that's so very important. She can talk to the dolly and the dolly will always listen. Dolly is never too busy and never distracted. Dolly doesn't disagree and doesn't interrupt.

Dolly is kinda well-worn, but in her own simple way, she's beautiful.

Well, Joy may have her dolly, but Jesse has his wood scraps. You know, old eight-inch-long two-by-fours and leftover pieces of half-inch pine from the shelves and plywood by the ton in every imaginable shape.

Jesse loves the stuff.

He gets out there in the garage with hammer, nails, paints, crayons, and markers and goes to town. He's created more works of art than Rembrandt. He's proud of them, too! He displays them on a special shelf in his room. What looked like scraps of discarded wood are translated into sea monsters, spaceships, motorcycles, and four-man bobsleds.

Okay, the art is a little on the primitive side, but in its own simple way, it's beautiful.

Jeffrey is the first son eligible for boys' hand-me-downs. He gets stuff Jesse no longer uses. Jeffrey's current inheritance is an old two-wheeler bicycle with training wheels. It's not real flashy . . . actually it's sorta old, faded, and rusty.

But that bike is the love of Jeffrey's life.

I've never seen him more freed up than when he's on that bike. He rides up and down the block, hair blowing in the breeze, singing, talking to no one, smiling, cheering, drinking in all of the freshness of life as a child.

A simple, hand-me-down bike . . . a beautiful sight.

John is the scholar in the family. He's not yet two and already reading. Not *reading* reading, but good, solid, one-year-old, picture-book reading. He has this forty-nine-cent Sesame Street book that is almost welded to his little body. He must read it thirty times a day.

John loves that beat-up old book.

When he wakes up in the morning, he reads it in his crib. He reads it during meals in his high chair. He reads it while sitting on the sofa, coffee table, kitchen counter, front porch step, and would probably read in the tub if we'd let him.

The pages are torn, ragged-edged, stained, and yellowed with age. But in its own simple way, that little book is beautiful.

Yes, baby dolls, blocks of wood, bikes, and books teach me the beauty of the simple life and the simplicity of the beautiful life.

Maybe that's what Christ was thinking of when He said, " . . . Observe how the lilies of the field grow; they do not toil nor do they spin, yet I say to you that even Solomon in all his glory did not clothe himself like one of these" (Matthew 6: 28,29).

So don't push so hard in your run for the roses that you forget to linger at the lilies.

You'll miss their simplicity . . . and their beauty.

Bb

Beauty is found in the simple things.

Making It Stick

Here's a very heavy project . . . are you ready? Make a plan to accomplish this project within the next two weeks. Mark it on your calendar. Don't allow anything to keep you from this appointment, okay! Here it is . . .

. . . play with your kids.

That's right—play with 'em. Not pray, *play* (we'll address praying later). It'll be a real education for you.

There are some rules, however. The first rule is: Don't run the show. You play what the kids want to play. They make the decisions. You'll love it.

The second rule is to make careful mental note of their choice of play. See, that's how I discovered the beauty of a well-worn cloth dolly, discarded two-by-four scraps, a rusty two-wheeler with training wheels, and a beat-up old book.

The last rule is: Evaluate your playtime once it concludes to see how "in-touch" you are with your kids. Could you have picked their favorite toys? Did you fall into the trap of big bucks for some expensive toy only to see the child play with the box in which it came? What lessons in beauty and simplicity did you discover?

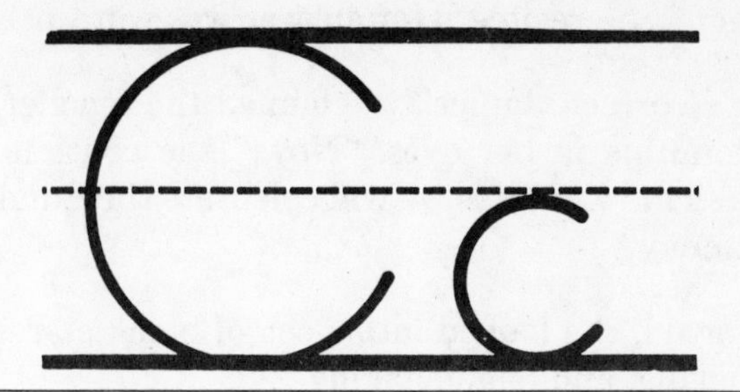

Children's Theology

I recently heard a story about a preschool-age Sunday school class. It seems that it was two weeks before Easter and the teacher was doing her best to arouse interest and excitement in the most sacred of all Christian holidays.

Fortunately for all stories such as these, there is always one member of the class who knows what is going on. More than likely, the member is a little girl, because little girls receive lots of positive reinforcement by just being cute, while little boys get negative reinforcement, because they misbehave to get some attention.

Anyway, the teacher asked the class a simple question: "Does anyone know what it is that we will celebrate next Sunday?" While the rest of the class sat stunned, our one bright little girl promptly raised her hand. The teacher called on her for the answer.

"Next Sunday is Palm Sunday, the day Jesus rode into Jerusalem," she recited. Her answer was word perfect.

"That's correct, Janice!" exclaimed the teacher, excitement mounting in her eyes. "Now," she continued, "can anyone tell me what it is we will celebrate the Sunday after Palm Sunday?"

Once again, she looked into a sea of blank stares, shoulder shrugging, and head shaking.

Except for you-know-who.

The teacher acknowledged the lifted hand of our little answer-woman. She promptly responded, "The Sunday after Palm Sunday is Easter Sunday."

Well, the teacher should've left well enough alone, but she pushed it further. "What happened on Easter, Janice? Do you know?"

"Oh, yes, teacher," replied Janice. "Easter is when Jesus Christ rose from the grave . . . "

"That's right!" interrupted the teacher. But Janice wasn't finished.

"Yes, and when Jesus comes out of the grave, if He sees His shadow, He goes back in for six more weeks. But if He doesn't see His shadow, He stays out!"

One fine example of children's theology.

There is probably no more demanding test of your communication skill than the challenge of communicating to children.

My kids often accompany me when I speak somewhere and they have come to realize that one of my favorite Bible characters is Moses. I love to tell the story of his leadership of the children of Israel. I particularly enjoy the account of the exodus from Egypt, climaxed at the Red Sea. It's quite an inspiring look at how God can help us through impossible situations.

Once I was driving home from a speaking occasion Jesse had attended with me. I had spoken on Moses leading the children of Israel through the Red Sea. Jess had heard the message three or four times, but he had one of those quizzical looks on his face.

"Dad," he began, "when Moses took the children of Israel through the Red Sea, did you say they walked across?"

"Well, yes, son," I answered. "That was the result of the miracle. The land was dry enough for them to walk on."

"But why didn't the children of Israel ride their Big Wheels?"

Bingo. It hit me. The *children* of Israel.

Here's a poor kid, having to hear the same message three or four times, yet each time his mental image is of over 2 million KIDS following one big Daddy—Moses, out of Egypt.

Children are literalists. They keep us on our toes (figuratively and sometimes, literally). Let's not lose them in some Gospel gumbo that they'll never understand. Let's tell it straight to our kiddos in a way they'll understand.

Moses didn't run a giant day-care center.

Christ is not a groundhog.

Cc

Communicate to your kids on their level... even when you talk about God.

Making It Stick

Get out your calendars and tell the family that on one particular evening next week, they're going to participate in a special event. Each person in the family should prepare to tell the rest of the family a Bible story. (Give them a time limit appropriate for their age.) If you want, allow one or two kids to work together. Maybe they'll want to dramatize a Bible story, read it, tell it in their own words, use pictures, flannel graphs, puppets, music, paints, or crayons.

Encourage creativity. Be supportive, encouraging, and available during the week as a resource person.

Make the actual evening as special as possible. Dim the lights between stories, dress up, be sure there's lots of applause and bravos.

You'll learn an awful lot from an evening like this. You may have a fine young Bible teacher on your hands . . . or you may have all new material for *your* chapter on Children's Theology.

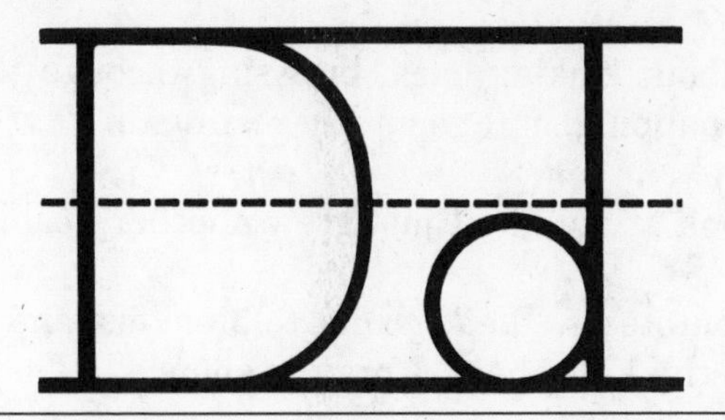

Days of Rest

Saturday is the day of rest. It's the time for the hardworking man to kick back and enjoy a lazy day around the house. You know, sleep in late (remember, tomorrow it's up early to get the kids ready for church), don't shave, browse through the paper, nap in front of the tube, snack, rest up for the busy week ahead. It's even godly! Genesis 2 tells us that God rested on the seventh day.

If resting on Saturday is godly . . . boy, am I a heathen!

Saturdays don't work like that at our house. "Sleeping in late" averages out to approximately 17.3 seconds more sleep than a weekday. My eyes sleepily focus in on a two-year-old, walking around on the nightstand, getting ready to . . . I'm out of bed.

The other kids are up too, watching Saturday morning cartoons. "You shouldn't watch that stuff," I mumble. "You'll grow up to be a menace to society."

"Whatta ya wanna do today, Dad?" they ask.

"How about kicking back, browsing through the paper, snacking, napping, and generally resting up?"

They look at me like I just grew another head.

Mom volunteers, "Let's go out to breakfast and then to a park!" All the kids cheer. I pray in silence to God.

I'm tempted to dress in scuba gear, knowing that whenever we eat out, liquid spills by the gallons. I just slip into an old shirt and jeans that I may never to able to wear again.

We notice a sudden hush falls over the restaurant as our troops march in. This is followed by people gulping food and asking for their checks. All we can conclude is that they've been in a restaurant with us before.

The kids bring little toys along to keep them busy while waiting for the food. Yet when the food comes, the toys don't disappear. Trucks turn up in the French toast, dolls in the juice, and worst of all, E.T. in the coffee.

After breakfast we go home, change into dry clothes, and head for the park. Ah, what rest! There's nothing as peaceful as the six-year-old daring the five-year-old to jump off the top of the monkey bars. There's nothing as relaxing as the two-year-old curiously examining the pond . . . from the middle of it. There's nothing as laid back as watching your nine-month-old dive into the sand box and try to eat its contents.

Home again after our park adventure, the older two go out on their bikes, the younger two settle in for an afternoon nap. That's not a bad idea!

"Finally," sighs my wife. "Let's get into that garage and clean it from top to bottom." I look at her like *she* just grew another head.

Saturday is the only time she has for those types of projects. After all, she lives with these troops twenty-four hours a day. At least I get eight hours off a day.

So we work like mad at reorganizing the garage. Our goal is to get a car into it. We're getting close. But then I start to wear down. "Is it Monday yet?" I ask.

That night I collapse into a chair. Suddenly, I realize that in a few short hours it will be Sunday morning. Wow! That means getting four kids fed, scrubbed, dressed, and smiling in time for Sunday school. Not too early . . . they'll get messed up. Not too late . . . we want a parking place.

It's those moments of meditation late Saturday night that help me realize that there will be plenty of Saturdays for "rest" down the road. I'm young. I'm healthy. I can get by without that kind of rest right now in my life.

A day will come when I'll yearn for cartoons, carousels, and cleaning. And it will be in the past. So I'm going to get all the satisfaction I can out of those times with my family. I'll sleep at a later date.

As a matter of fact, I'm reserving the year 2004 entirely for sleep. By then, I'll need it.

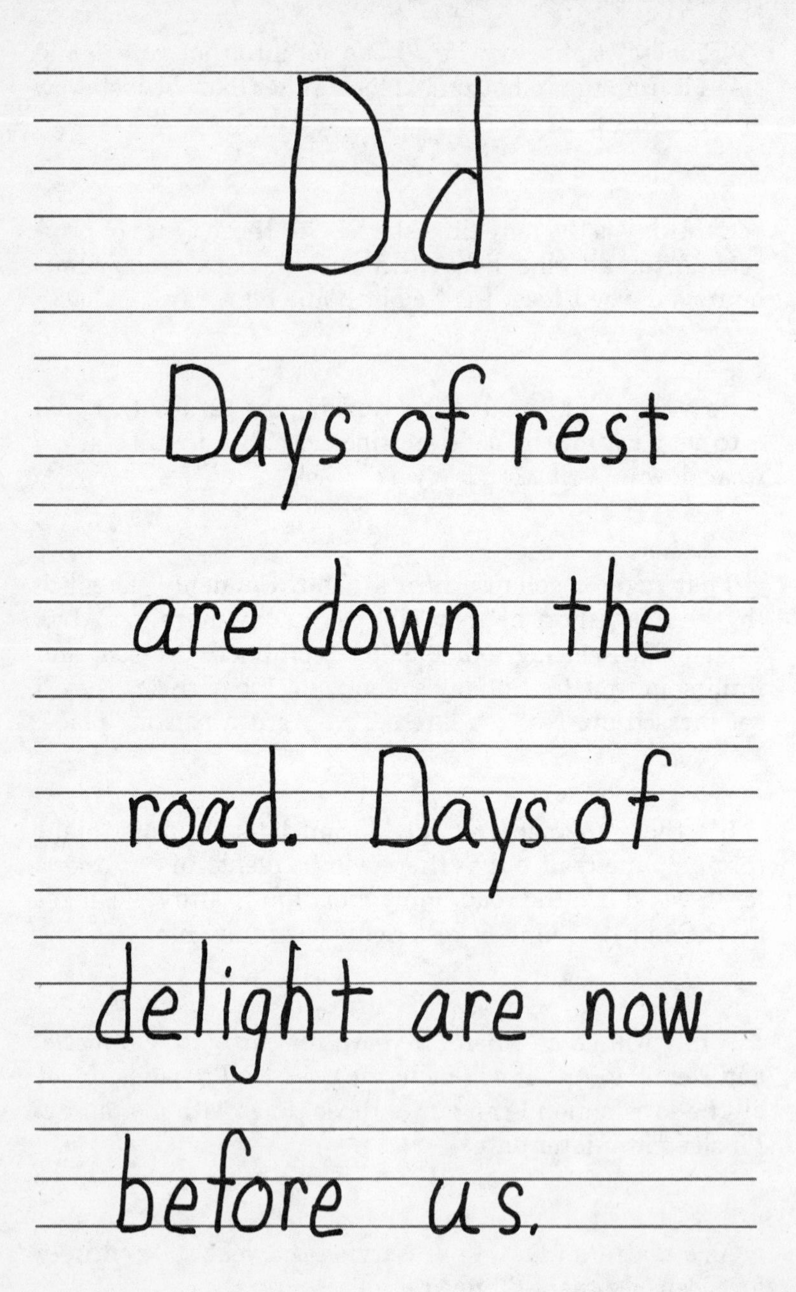
Dd
Days of rest
are down the
road. Days of
delight are now
before us.

Making It Stick

How would you describe your day of rest? Is it similar to mine? Find a pencil and some paper and chart out a *typical* day off. (I know they all seem different, but force yourself to come up with a good representation of a day off.)

Now, next to each activity of the day, write in the central character. For example, if it's going to the park it's *the kids*, if it's fixing your wife's sewing machine, it's *your wife*. It may be one particular child, or a friend, neighbor, or, of course, *yourself*.

So how does it look? Balanced? Are you spending a fair amount of time with each particular member of your family? Take the last few minutes to figure out how you would *like* it to be. What can you do in the next few weeks to make those changes? Commit this whole project to God and ask Him to help you make these days of rest, days of delight.

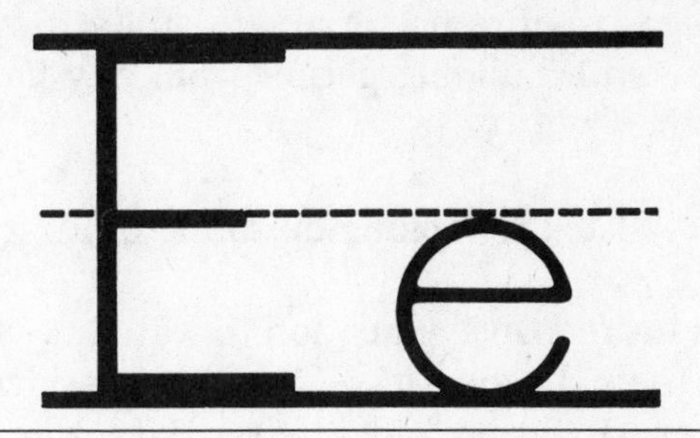

Exploding Legos

Part of the job description for a younger brother goes something like this: "You must look up to your older brother and demonstrate this through acts of loyalty and frequent imitation."

Styles have changed. Clothes have changed. Toys have changed. But looking up to big brother has remained immutable.

When I was a kid, the big thing in building blocks was a hot item called Lincoln Logs. They were sticks of wood with three-quarter-inch grooves on the ends so that you could construct a replica of Abe Lincoln's log cabin. Today, Lincoln Logs have been replaced by Legos. With Legos, you don't build replicas of the home of the sixteenth president, instead you build replicas of homes for presidents not yet born.

Now, I admit to a little prejudice, but Lincoln Logs were for kids. Legos require postgraduate study in mechanical engineering and a building permit from city hall. But my kids love 'em.

Anyway . . . back to looking up to big brother.

It was an inexpensive education to watch my three boys play with their Legos. Jesse was the resident master craftsman at six years old. Jeffrey was the struggling three-year-old apprentice. John was one year old and just learning that Legos weren't for lunch.

Jesse would get an idea and go with it. He'd see a picture of a Lego Lunar Landing Module and start in on the building process. Naturally, when Jeffrey observed Jesse's choice of construction, he would immediately start in on his own version of the Lego Lunar Landing Module.

Imitation may be the sincerest form of flattery, but it's also the fastest flight to frustration.

You see, Jesse had some advantages over Jeffrey. Things like better eye-hand coordination, greater development of the small muscles in the hands and fingers, motor skills with more maturity.

In other words, Jesse worked peacefully while Jeffrey popped his cork.

Carefully mimicking his brother, Jeffrey was just fine for about five bricks. Then he'd hit that one little brick that wouldn't fit on the rest. He'd panic, then press it down as hard as he could. It wouldn't lock. He frantically looked at how his brother was now way ahead in the space race. His frustration level kept rising. His face reddened, his hands got sweaty, his mouth got dry.

The proverbial cool was about to be lost as Jeffrey carefully gathered all the Legos he could fit into his pudgy little paws. Then, in a procedure similar to the eruptions at Mount Saint Helens, he threw all the Legos straight up in the air, spreading them all over the room, accompanied by the deafening roar of defeat—

"AAAAAAAAAAAAAAAAAAAHHHHHHHH!!!!"

Being short on patience he had the first of what we now refer to at our house as a "Lego Explosion."

But I realized something in all this. I realized that I am a master of "Mental Lego Explosions." As my patience grows thin, the blocks go flying through the air to the corners of my mind. I frequently erupt, complete with red face, sweaty hands, and dry mouth. Jeffrey's Lego Explosions are mirrors of myself.

So, maybe Jeffrey wasn't imitating his brother.

Maybe he was imitating me.

Baby John learned how to imitate too. He learned how to play with Legos by watching Jeffrey.

He didn't build with Legos. He just picked them up, threw them high into the air, and shrieked out in his own one-year-old style—

"AAAAAAAAAAAAAAAAAAAHHHHHHHH!!!!"

Like father . . . like sons.

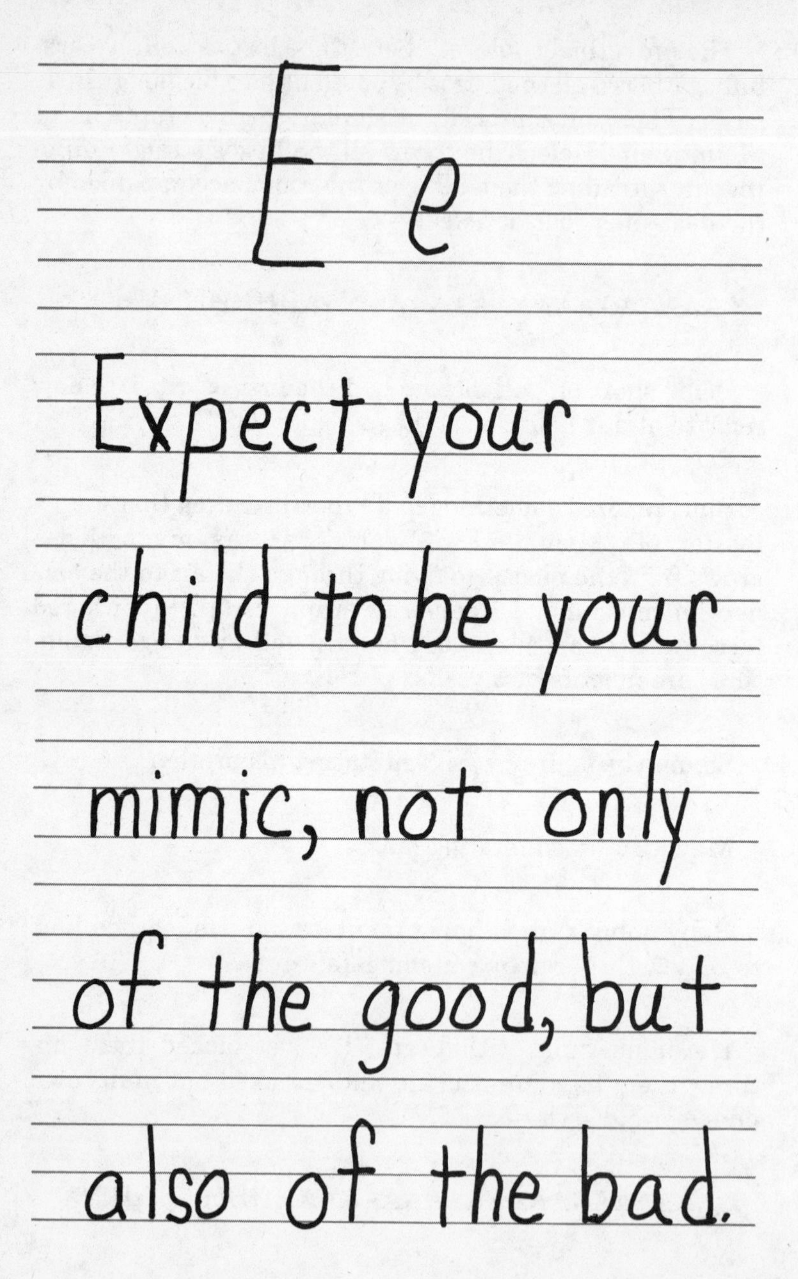
Ee
Expect your
child to be your
mimic, not only
of the good, but
also of the bad.

Making It Stick

Kids are like that, aren't they? There's something inside them that makes them incredible mimics. But it's not always cute. Sometimes it's painful.

Grab some paper, pencil, coffee, and your mate (in any order). Write the names of your children, one to a page. Talk to each other about their ability to mimic. What does your oldest do that reminds you of your mate? Or reminds you of yourself? Let your spouse get a word in here or there.

Go through this process for each of your kids. When you're finished you ought to have quite a list! Now, go back over your list and put a star (☆) by those traits that are *desirable* in your child. Put a check (√) by those *undesirable* characteristics.

Discuss this together. Remember, since these are traits of a mimic, the way to produce change is to work on the ***model***! In case you missed it, that's you!

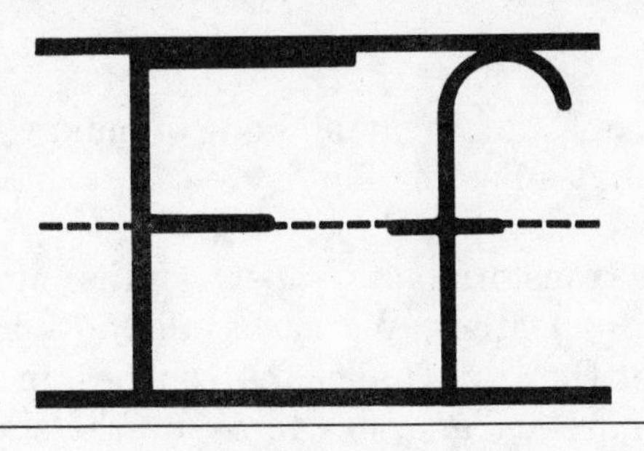

Finder of Lost Gloves

All adults benefit greatly from the five senses they've been given by God. But when adults become parents, it would be good to be able to develop a sixth sense. This particular sense would help them with their sanity, keep them closer to being on time for appointments, and save them big bucks in the long haul.

I'm referring, of course, to the sixth sense of "finding lost items around the house."

You know the scene: You're frantically rushing around, dressing the little ones in order to be on time for your son's Little League game. You nervously glance at your watch and discover you're actually a little ahead of schedule!

All the little ones are washed, dressed, and buckled in the car, ready to go. It is then that your Little Leaguer utters the words that alter the course of history.

"MOM! DAD! I CAN'T FIND MY BASEBALL GLOVE!!!"

With that one statement, all hope of making the start of the game is but a fleeting fantasy.

So we all transform into super sleuths, attempting to find a lump of leather. We check all the normal hiding places: under the beds, under the couches, in the closets, behind the bureaus, and, of course, on the shelf where it belongs. Sooner or later we find the glove where it would most logically rest after a long, hot practice . . .

. . . in the refrigerator.

"Oh yeah," sighs Jesse. "After practice I came in to get some cold water and since I couldn't hold the water and the glove, I left the glove in the 'frigerator so I wouldn't spill my drink."

I've never seen a baseball glove that said "Refrigerate after opening."

Then there was the memorable Friday night we were packing up to go off for a weekend conference where I was to speak on "Harmonious Family Relationships."

Packing for two adults and four children for two days and an overnight is a challenge for any human being. Since I hate to be selfish with challenges, I allow Rhonda to pack for everyone, thus permitting her to share in the adventure of living.

It was about eight-thirty Friday evening when we discovered we could only find *one* of John's tennis shoes. One shoe was missing.

"I know where it is!" Joy announced. "It's out in the front yard!"

We have an outside light on the porch, but it does no good when you must search every inch of your front yard for a tennis shoe the size of a credit card.

So out came the flashlights. Of course the batteries are old so we have the equivalent of one and a half candles out on the front lawn. I'm down on my hands and knees scouring the area, but to no avail.

Three baseball cards, an old tennis ball, a nozzle to a hose, and thirty-seven cents in loose change, but no tennis shoe.

"Maybe," Joy pondered, "I saw it in the neighbor's lawn."

So we moved our traveling circus to the next lot, but again, no luck.

It's one thing to attend a conference with a child who has only one shoe. It's quite different, however, when you are the speaker.

Now you know how my kids get new shoes. It's generally nine-thirty at night, just as the stores are closing. One frantic father passes a single shoe to a wearied worker and says, "Match this, please."

But the Grand Prize for Most Frequently Lost Items has to go to the two blankets carried around everywhere by my two youngest, Jeffrey and John. Their blankets have been lost more times than is humanly possible to remember.

I've found those blankets in trees, under cars, in the frozen food section of grocery stores, under a seat in Dodger Stadium, and, if you can believe this, in a restaurant that was being evacuated during a large grease fire in the kitchen.

Both blankets bear the scars of being on the road full-time with preschoolers. They've both had everything imaginable spilled on them. They've been frozen, thawed, rained on, baked in the sun, ripped, wet on, and most of all, loved to death.

Well, life sure would be a lot simpler without gloves, tennis shoes, and blankets.

But life would be a lot simpler without kids, too. Yet, every time one gets lost, I can't wait till he's found!

Ff

Families that
find together,
bind together.

Making It Stick

How about a fun evening for the family? Gather the family together in the family room or out on the patio and spend an hour or two swapping detective stories. Let Mom recount how she found Junior's T-shirt in the fruit salad. Then let Sis share how she found her brother's toothbrush in her set of encyclopedias. Dad will want to share about losing the *TV Guide*, only to find it a week later (when it's out of date) in the dryer. You'll be pleasantly surprised at how even the little ones will join right in with their own stories.

Wrap up your good time with some special goodies. The only trick is . . . if your kids want 'em, they're going to have to find 'em! Finders Keepers, Losers Hungry.

By the way, if you think you have a problem about losing things, cheer up. By now, someone has already lost his copy of this book and you're still reading yours!

Gorilla

Her name is Charissa Nelson.

She is part of an elite group of female commandos. It's kind of a Southern California version of the Green Berets. The requirements are physically demanding, emotionally draining, intellectually fatiguing, and spiritually excruciating. Frankly, there are only a few brave women qualified for this life-or-death mission. No starry-eyed junior highers would do here. And there is no finer example than Charissa Nelson. What do we call this mighty band of wonder women?

Butterworth's Baby-sitters.

Charissa comes from good stock. Her mom and dad are Cynthia and Chuck Swindoll. They taught her everything they could about survival. Her husband, Byron, is a man who knows how fortunate he is to have such a special lady.

So when she is asked over to baby-sit, he quickly reviews karate with her and sends her off as well prepared as she can be.

One evening, however, when Rhonda and I returned from a night out, there was something distinctively different in the air. The usually neat and tidy Charissa looked like a hurricane survivor.

Her blonde hair was unkempt and disheveled. Her eyes were watering. Her face was flushed. Most notably, her blouse was torn and she practically had to hold it together.

"What happened?" we gasped, thinking the worst.

"I—I played with—with the kids," she stammered. *"Gorilla!"*

"Oh," we sighed with relief, slumped down into our chairs, and started laughing. "We forgot to tell you—don't *ever* play Gorilla with the kids. That's a special game for them and their daddy."

"I see," mumbled Charissa, still barely audible. "Now I know."

But don't worry, folks. After some coffee, Band-Aids, washcloths, needle and thread, and true compassion, we were able to bring Charissa back to strong normal health.

Since I've gone this far, I might as well answer the big question: What in the world is Gorilla, anyway?

Well, it's something real special for the kids and me (and the kids and Charissa *once*). The term that would best describe Gorilla to anyone not in our immediate family would be good old all-American WRESTLING.

Yes, when we play Gorilla, Daddy gets down on the living room rug, takes off his glasses, takes off his shirt (I used to take off my T-shirt, too, but they never wanted to wrestle then—they would just laugh and point), and makes sounds like King Kong. We roll around the living room, doing flips, getting tickled, enjoying free piggyback rides, giving and receiving bear hugs, and experiencing the enjoyment only wrestling can bring.

I think every dad should have his own version of Gorilla. For one thing, it's PHYSICAL. You know how valuable your touch is to your child. What a great excuse for fifteen minutes of uninterrupted physical contact. Second, it's SPECIAL. Something just for you and your kids. See, that was Charissa's mistake and our oversight. She unknowingly got conned into a game even their mother wouldn't play with them! Make it exclusive—no other dads—no other kids.

Charissa learned some valuable lessons on that memorable evening. I'm sure as Byron and she begin their family, Byron will have his own rendition of wrestling with the kids.

But the immediate lesson for Charissa was: Let baby-sitters be baby-sitters and let daddies be animals.

After all, baby-sitting shouldn't be "gorilla warfare."

(By the way, Charissa is recounting this tale of terror in her new book *Baby-sitting for the Planet of the Apes.*)

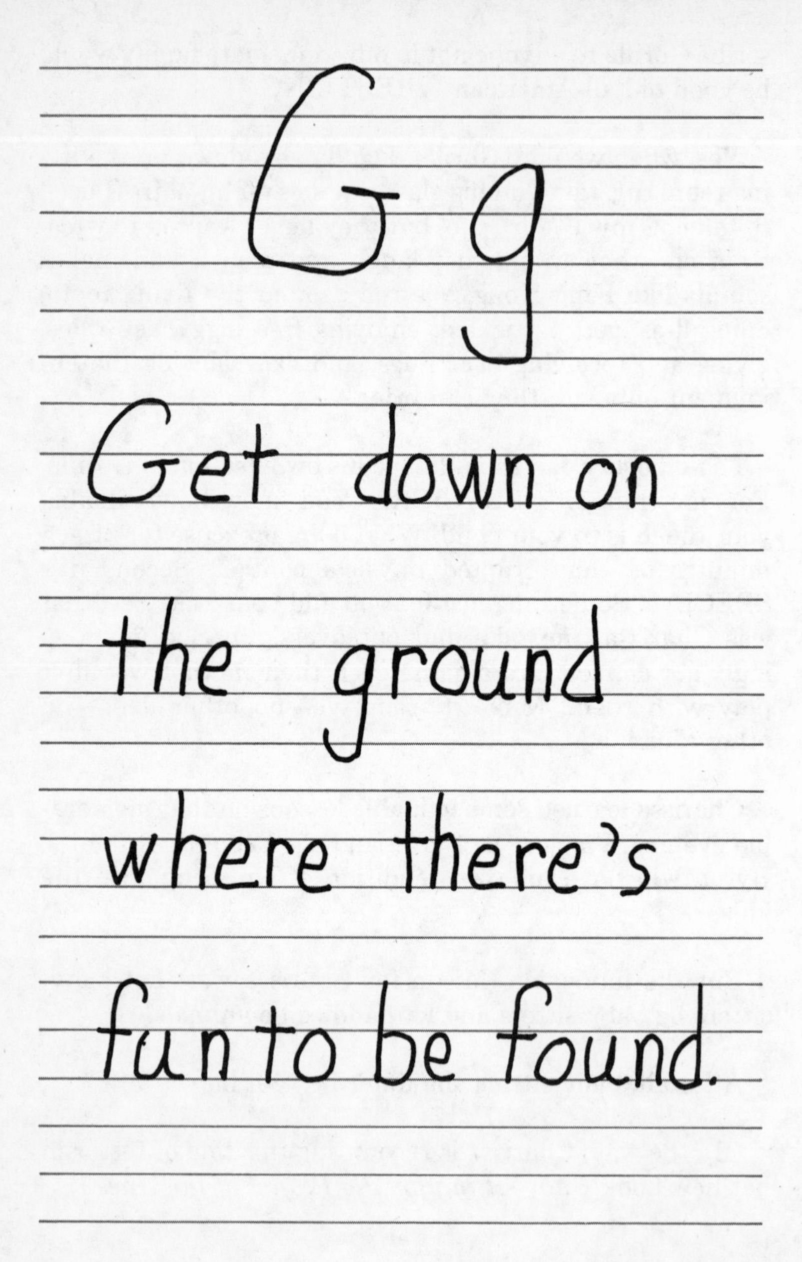
Gg
Get down on
the ground
where there's
fun to be found.

Making It Stick

Dads, what's the Gorilla in your life? What is there in your relationship with your children that allows them to see the fun side of Dad?

Let's probe this even further. What are you doing to insure some physical contact between you and your children? Some dads are naturally more "touch-oriented" than others, so some will find this question easy to answer, others won't know where to begin.

But let's get specific by thinking through a contact plan. Look for easy leaks and plug them up—with hugs and kisses when you leave for work, when you return home, at bedtime, and, best of all, for no reason.

Moms, help Dad become the Big Ape he was intended to be. Work as a team to bring this important dimension into your family's lives.

Celebrate with a Gorilla Party. What to serve? What else?

Bananas.

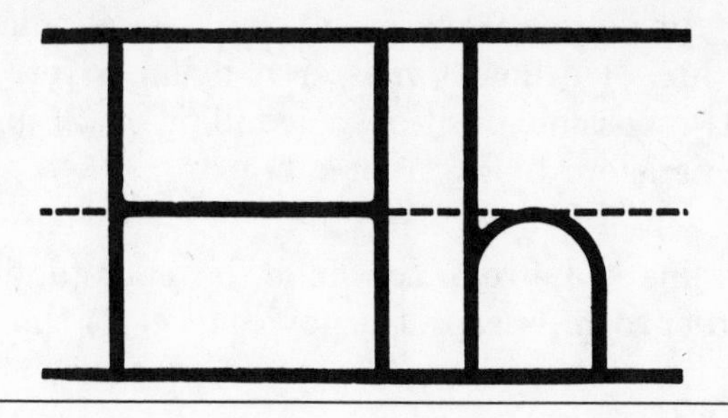

Healthy Growth

When you think of measuring growth, you usually think in terms of rulers, tape measures, or yardsticks. Well, at our place, I have my own way of mapping out the intangible aspects of growth. It's different, but effective. How do I measure growth?

Roller skates.

Yes, roller-skating has swept our family of little ones. All four of them hit the sidewalks first thing in the morning and don't come inside till dark, unless there's bleeding or bruising beyond belief.

Each child is at a different level of skating expertise—that's why I can measure growth. Joy is our oldest and she skates like a champ. She knows every crack and crevice in our local sidewalks, so she rarely loses her balance. She's even working on some stunts!

Jesse, the next oldest is still in the early stages of skating. He's the kind of skater who gives you ulcers just watching him. He hasn't mastered balance yet. Skating takes on two possible positions: (1) falling or (2) just about to fall. Jesse is our black 'n' blue boy.

Next in line is Jeffrey. You have to understand skating lingo in order to appreciate the novice level for this guy. To state it in its simplest terms:

Jeffrey skates in the grass.

That way there's no such thing as speed. It's slow city on the lawn. Also, if you can possibly fall moving three feet an hour, you'll fall on the nice soft dirt rather than cruel cold concrete.

Baby John has his own unique approach. He's too young to skate, technically speaking, but that doesn't discourage him in the least.

He puts the skates on his hands and crawls down the sidewalk.

Roller-skating illustrates growth to me. But the skates just scratch the surface.

Growth is a popular topic in our household. The kids want to grow bigger and faster and taller and older. Mom and Dad are content just to remain in a holding pattern. At the dinner table I asked the kids what they wanted to be when they grew up. Joy said, "A nurse or a teacher or a waitress." Jesse said, "A preacher, a fire-truck man, or the 'Credible' Hulk!" Jeffrey wants to be a refrigerator. John grunts.

One thing I try to teach them is that growth is a *process*. Even with all our scientific technology, we've been unable to invent a potion that causes instant growth. That tends to rub us the wrong way, since we can solve any problem in sixty minutes with four commercial breaks.

Another observation I've made is that growth has *spurts and lags*. Like in the seventh grade when the girls are ten inches taller than the boys and the boys compensate by having feet long enough for barefoot skiing. But what happens in the next few years? The gals grow only an inch or two and the guys are drafted by the Lakers. The reason? We all have our own personal times of growth that *may* follow a basic pattern but are very individually experienced.

So even though growth has its spurts and lags, the process continues. It won't be long till John skates as well as Joy. My job is to provide an atmosphere that encourages healthy growth.

Just in case I forget the importance of growth, God has given me roller skates as a visual reminder, an object lesson of that concept. Every time I see a skate I'm reminded of the importance of growth.

Sometimes I don't even have to see the skate in order to be reminded . . .

. . . like late last night when I *discovered* that skate left in our darkened hallway.

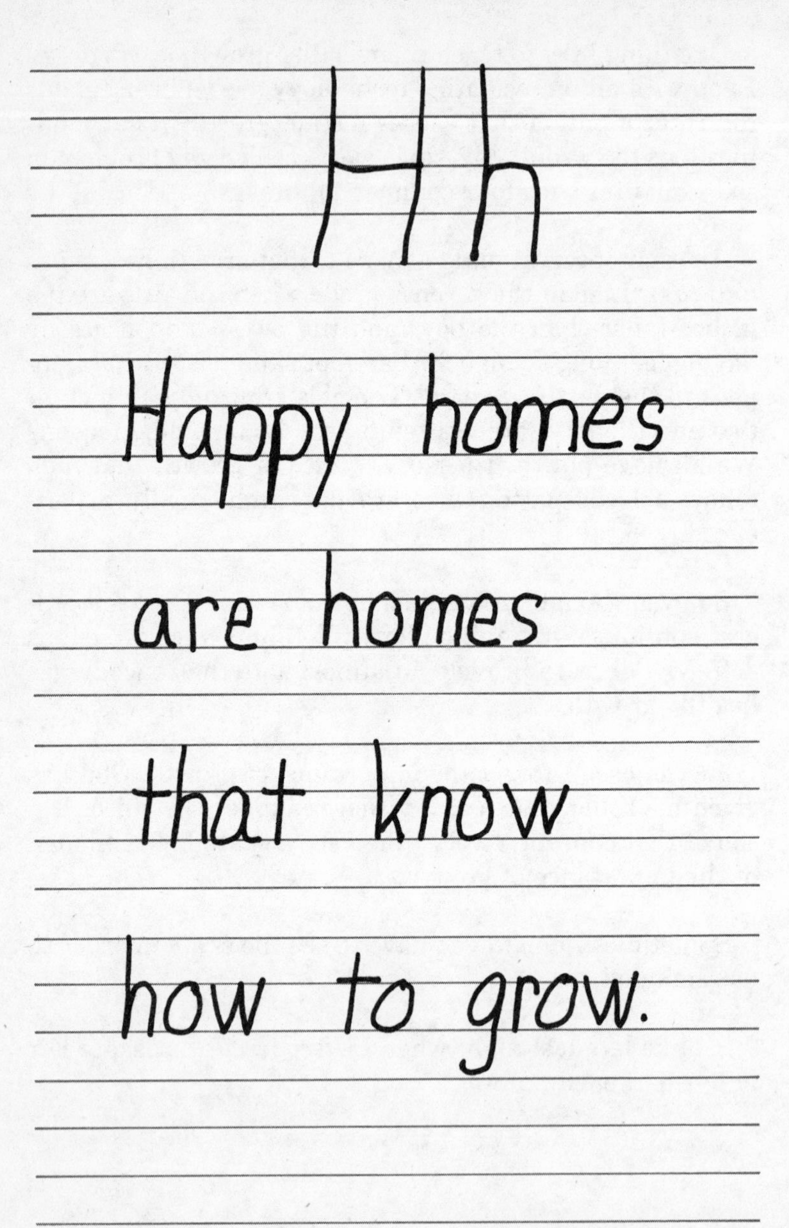
Hh
Happy homes
are homes
that know
how to grow.

Making It Stick

Growth is an integral part of every person's life. And healthy growth is a goal we should seek to achieve. In the Scriptures, it is called maturity in Christ. Either way you look at it, it's essential.

As parents, here's a warm way to reflect on growth. Raid the closets, shelves, boxes, and drawers and dig up the old PHOTO ALBUMS and SCRAPBOOKS. Snuggle up with one another on the couch and review the growth of your children. Let your thoughts weave their ways to your mouth and thus "talk through" the lives of your kids.

What's this process of child raising been all about in your home? Has it been a healthy environment? Is it getting better every day? Is maturity occurring on all levels?

Some of you will talk deep into the night. That's just fine. True, it'll make for a rough day after, but perhaps it will lead to an even better tomorrow because of healthy growth.

Inside the Garage

Every red-blooded American male yearns for real adventure. I'm talking about high adventure ... like in the movies. When I get that kind of urge, I get into the appropriate attire. I slip into khaki shorts, matching bush jacket, knee socks, hiking boots, and, of course, pith helmet. I strap to my side my trusty tools of survival: machete, revolver, Swiss army knife, whip, and two granola bars.

By now my blood is tingling with the raw anticipation of jungle intrigue. I take one last check of the equipment. Everything's in order. Finally, I announce my plans ...

" ... I'm off to clean out the garage," I announce in somber tones.

Rhonda and the kids just shake their heads. They know that this adventure takes place once a year . . . springtime to be exact. And every year it gets worse. But the kids always volunteer to come along.

I blame it on the lawn. If it didn't grow, it wouldn't need mowing. And if it didn't need mowing, I wouldn't need the lawn mower. And if I didn't need the lawn mower, I wouldn't have to clean out the garage in order to find it.

Every winter it gets buried in a garage full of junk. My garage has never seen my car. We'd need something akin to parting the Red Sea for that to ever happen.

But the kids absolutely love the adventure of examining all the treasures hidden in the four corners of this tiny room. Finding a lawn mower is just a good excuse for having a lot of fun.

Does my garage sound like your garage? Here's a partial list of what I had to move out in order to get to the lawn mower:

- Two lamps—one with shade, one without
- A nightstand moved out of a bedroom for more space
- Seven 4 × 4 beams to be used for replacement fence posts
- A serving cart, once used in the kitchen of Marabel Morgan
- An artificial Christmas tree
- Three 90-lb. bags of cement for the fence posts
- An empty fish tank, abandoned by fish years ago
- A chest of drawers, jammed full of clothes from the '60s
- A record player in the shape of Scooby Doo
- One roll of linoleum weighing in at four tons

- A barbecue grill I forgot we had
- Enough 2 × 4s to rebuild Germany
- Five tricycles: Two with only two wheels
Two without handlebars
One without a seat
- Three bicycles: One with only one wheel
One without handlebars
One without a seat
- A screen door that looks like it came from Iwo Jima
- A toy box in the shape of Reggie Jackson
- The carpet we pulled up from our bedroom
- The bed frame of a bed in the shape of Bambi
- A box of shoes . . . enough to have shod all of China
- A set of old encyclopedias—endorsed by President Taft
- Twenty-three sheets of warped plywood
- Back issues of *Reader's Digest*—going back to May of '59
- Four boxes of pink baby clothes
- My collection of Beach Boys records
- Two bags of fertilizer—smelled that one comin'
- A stuffed squirrel
- The *original* vacuum cleaner owned by Van Vacuum himself
- One set of dishes . . . too good to use
- A nine-year supply of protein powder we got conned into buying
- A plaster of paris relief map of Boston
- An old sofa . . . once brown, now green
- A box of wedding presents . . . we save 'em to give at other weddings
- Two clock radios: one with broken radio, one with broken clock
- A box of pictures in need of frames
- A box of frames

- A box with Jeffrey in it . . . how long has he been in there?
- A grass catcher

"Kids, kids! I found the grass catcher! We're getting close. The lawn mower can't be too far away!"

I grabbed a set of handles. This was it! "Kids, . . . look, I've got the handles right here . . . this has to be it!" As they watched, they shared the joy of discovery with me. We pulled away the debris and, sure enough, there it was . . . an old floor polisher.

"Wait, kids, don't get discouraged. It's gotta be in here."

Well I finally found the lawn mower.

But no one was watching. Joy was playing with the four boxes of pink baby clothes. Jesse was attempting to read President Taft's encyclopedia endorsement. Jeffrey was petting the stuffed squirrel. John was making the five tricycles and three bicycles into an eighteen-wheeler semi.

I was just about to lecture them on the hazards of making a mess when I paused to look more closely into their faces. They were so excited about their discoveries. It reminded me of the first time I found my dad's army duffel bag from the days of World War II. It was magic.

So I allowed the discovering to continue. Some people dive deep into the sea for sunken treasures, others dig holes deep in the ground at the sign of the *X* on the Treasure Map.

But for my kids, the thrill of treasure is right outside their door . . .

. . . and inside the garage.

I i

Investigate
your family
treasures
real soon!

Making It Stick

For our family, it's the garage. For yours, it may be a basement, closet, attic, hope chest, old bureau, shed, or, of course . . . under the bed.

Whatever it is, how about planning a treasure hunt? Don't wait to lose the lawn mower as an excuse; get busy and plan a time to explore some uncharted section of your house, yard, or garage. As you plow through, pause to explain what each item is and what it represents.

Under "H" we looked at photos and scrapbooks reviewing the lives of our kids. Now, let's turn our attention to you, Mom and Dad!

Your kids love you, remember? They get exhilarated over finding out things about you, especially about when you were young. Maybe your parents can be of assistance in making this treasure hunt a valuable one. It's a great time, indeed, when the old year books, photo albums, record collections, clothes, and memorabilia find their way out of their hiding places and into the hearts of your children.

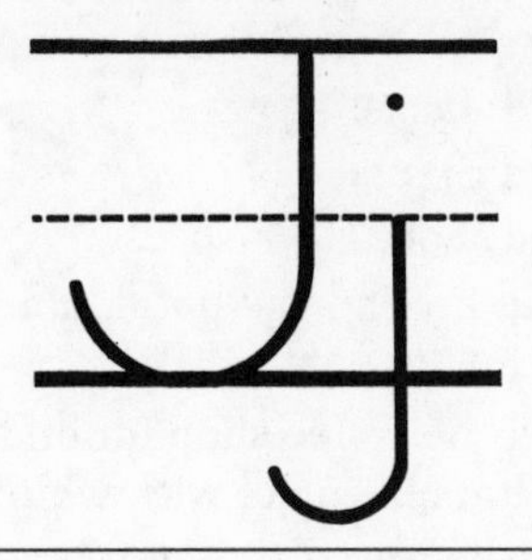

Joy's Funnest Day

My daughter and I just returned from the most spiritual Saturday we've ever spent together. I've gotta tell you about it. It was godly, spiritually enriching, Christ-honoring, God-glorifying, holy, biblically obedient, personally uplifting, and worshipfully spontaneous.

I was invited out of town to speak at a Saturday evening banquet.

I took Joy with me and arrived at the hotel early that morning. We checked in, met briefly with the banquet coordinator, and politely dismissed ourselves, agreeing to meet again at 6:20 P.M. for the banquet.

At that point we began our day of spiritual stuff. Here's a brief summary:

- We played the classic American game Go Fish (Joy's all-time favorite game).
- We played Jacks.
- We played Slapjack.
- We played more Go Fish.
- We walked around the hotel, holding hands.
- More Go Fish.
- We visited the coffee shop for one coffee and one large hot chocolate with whipped cream.
- Some high-powered tic-tac-toe.
- Go Fish.
- We walked down the street to a local gift shop. We found one gift each for the boys and Mama. Interestingly enough we found two gifts for Joy.
- We walked back to the hotel, trying not to step on the cracks in the sidewalk, since they were "Hot Lava" (or as one of Joy's younger brothers calls it "Ha Laba").
- Back to the room for Go Fish.
- Watched about twelve minutes of a basketball game on TV.
- Another stop at the coffee shop. This time for a scoop of orange sherbet to cool down from the large hot chocolate with whipped cream.
- Go Fish.
- A walk out to the hotel swimming pool in order to determine if it's warm enough to go swimming. Too cold.
- A race to the water fountain.
- A three-minute lesson on why the key for Room 274 won't open Room 278.
- Half a game of War interrupted by the desire to return to Go Fish.
- A phone call to Mama and the boys.
- A walk to the hotel's Pac-Man Machine to run an experiment . . . how many quarters

can an arcade game eat in twenty minutes?
- Return to the room $4.75 lighter.
- Start to get ready for the banquet.
- Go to the banquet. Joy will attempt to color six pictures in the time it takes for me to give my talk. She does it.
- Shake hands with every banquet attendee, waiter, waitress, busboy, bellman, and maintenance man.
- Return to hotel room to play one more game of Go Fish before bed. Joy gets ready for bed quicker than I do, so she lays in bed waiting for me. She makes the mistake of putting her head on the pillow. No Go Fish. She's zonked.
- I sit in silence, thanking God for the funnest day I've ever had with my daughter.

See, that's why it was so godly, so spiritual. It was so fun. I know what you're thinking. That with the exception of the banquet, we never cracked the Bible, sang a hymn, or quoted a verse. You're right. I'm not against any of these things. We do them often at our house, but on that particular day Joy and I had something different. There are days when the Bible is for *living*, not for reading.

The thing that happened that day was my little girl saw the Dad who loves her enough to discipline her, and the Dad who loves her enough to instruct her in the things of the Lord, is *also* the Dad who loves her enough to PLAY with her.

So, next time your child seems up to his ears in teaching, singing, or quoting, try this strategy:

Go have some sanctified fun.

It may be the best time the two of you ever have together.

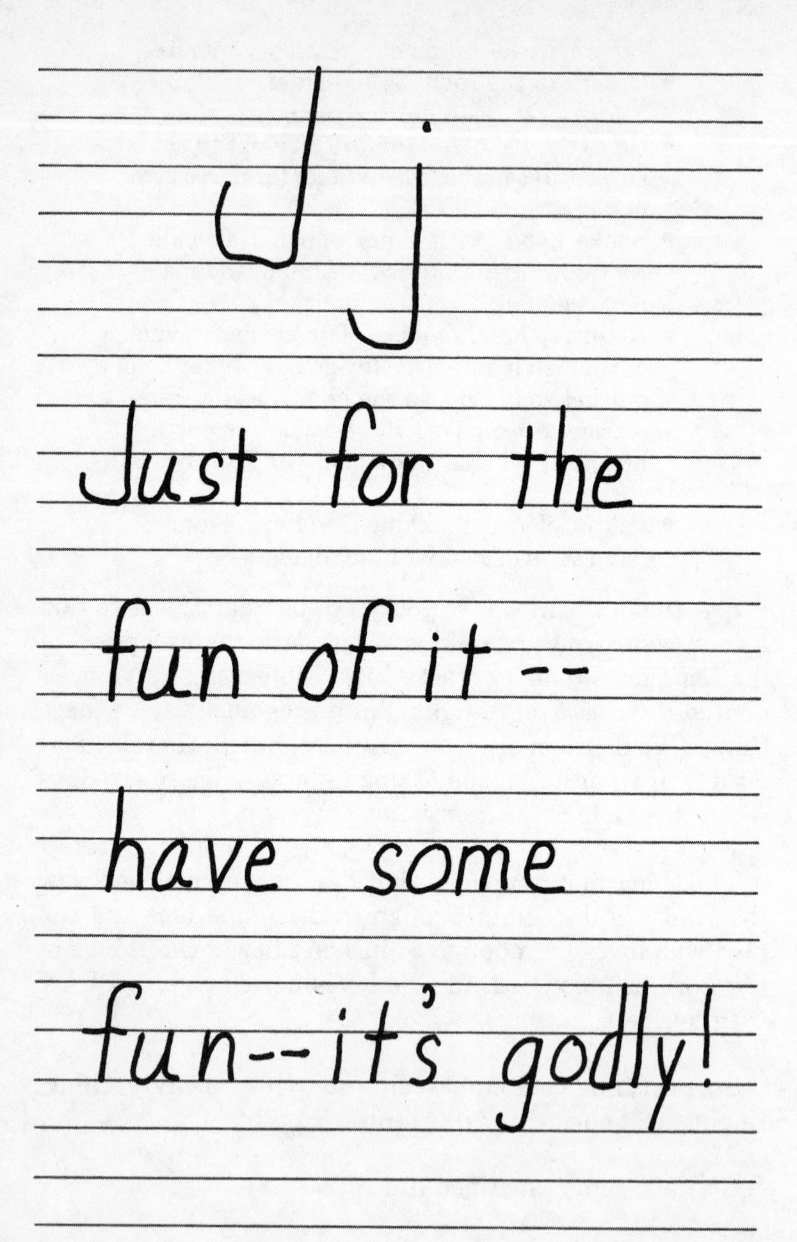
Jj
Just for the
fun of it --
have some
fun--it's godly!

Making It Stick

Joy and I were attending a father-daughter banquet some time ago. At that event, we were asked to share with one another *the* best time we ever had together as father and daughter. It was a tough assignment for both of us, because we've had a lot of great times together . . . trips to Disneyland or Sea World or Knott's Berry Farm or picnics, or beach days, or nature walks or ball games.

But *nothing* for just the two of us.

All of the above fun times were with the whole family!

Well, that's what did it for me. It was that banquet that convinced me of the need to take Joy with me on my speaking engagement a few weeks later. And it became our funnest day.

Write down the names of your kids and next to their names write down each one's funnest day ALONE with you. If answers don't come quickly, plan NOW a specific time and place for the solution.

Be sure to go beyond great ideas on paper, Mom and Dad. This funnest day stuff is serious business . . . let's see some action!

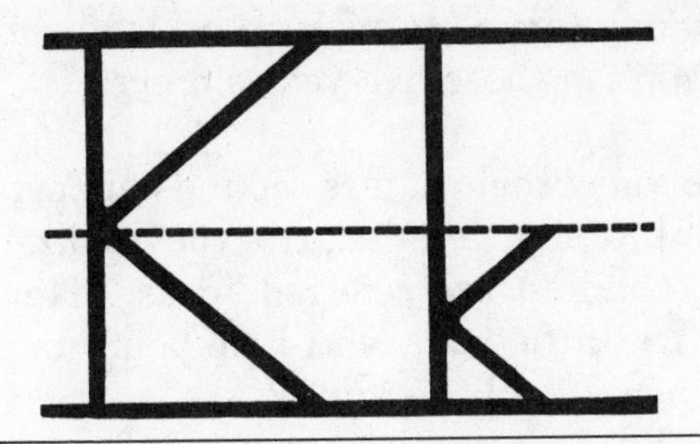

Kindergarten Keepsake

Who is the wisest person in the world?

Given all the world, and all of history, names like King Solomon, Galileo, or Albert Einstein are expected answers. But then again, you never get expected answers from kids.

When Jesse was five years old, the answer to that question was as easy as pie.

"The wisest person in all the world is Mrs. Green," Jesse replied without a moment's hesitation.

Mrs. Green was Jesse's kindergarten teacher.

And the more I think about it, he may be right.

See, Mrs. Green has taught kindergarten for over thirty-five years. She's got her act together. The kindergarteners know it and love her for it.

I had the occasion to watch her in action one day It didn't take long for me to pick up on why she's "World's Wisest Person" in those five-year-old eyes.

First, she knew their names. Sounds almost too silly to mention, but wait a minute. Do you realize how many times your children are referred to as, "Hey kid, come here!" or, "Yes, little boy, can I help you?" or even worse, "Get outta here, you little imp!"?

None of that for Mrs. Green. She calls them by their names. And boy, do they appreciate it.

Another trait I noticed is that she treated her class with respect. No one in that class of twenty-eight was seen as a helpless baby, but rather, a healthy discoverer.

Maybe Mrs. Green made it through all those years of kindergarten by allowing the kids to do a lot of her work for her. They loved taking attendance, cleaning the chalkboards, creating bulletin boards, lining up desks neatly in rows, and cleaning up after midmorning snack.

But perhaps the greatest thing going for Mrs. Green was her willingness to be flexible with her curriculum. She knew the value of capitalizing on the teachable moment.

For example, one rainy day the kids all arrived at school and noticed that during the thunder and lightning of the night before, one of the school's trees had been struck and was on its side in the playground.

Now you tell me, what does a kid want to do when there's a thirty-foot tree on its side in the playground? Play with clay? Color? Listen to a story? Yet most teachers would open their lesson plans and fight a losing battle against the playground's distraction.

Not Mrs. Green.

"Everybody bundle up in your rain gear, class! We're going to see what the inside of a tree looks like!"

There was total exhilaration in the class. They went nuts over their "field trip."

That's one wise lady.

We need more Mrs. Greens. Not only in the kindergarten classes, but in all other classes, and *anyplace* where adults interact with kids.

Including parents in the home.

Mrs. Green is retired now. But anybody who went through her class at Fern Drive Elementary School in Fullerton, California, has never forgotten the slice of her life that she passed on.

So move over Einstein. Mrs. Green is now on top of the list.

May her kind continue.

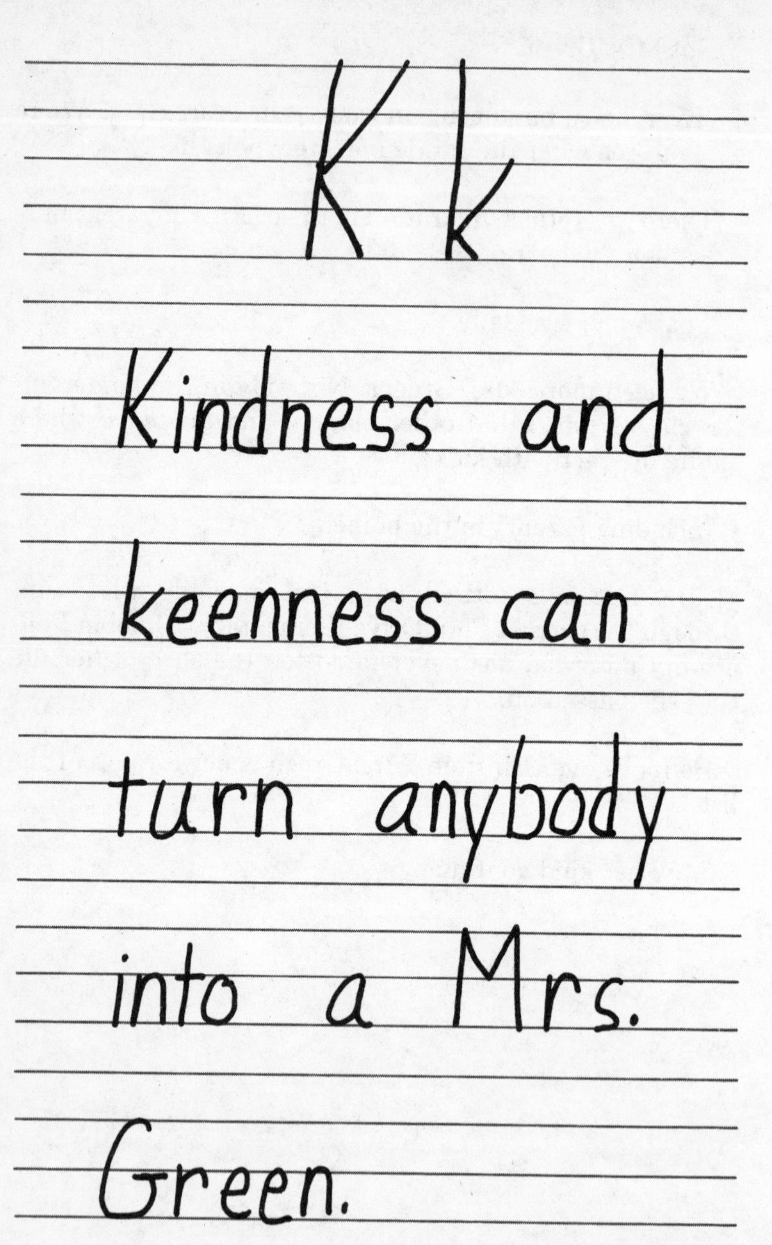
Kk
Kindness and
keenness can
turn anybody
into a Mrs.
Green.

Making It Stick

Mom and Dad, how do we rate, placed alongside Mrs. Green? Hopefully we all score well in knowing our child's name and using it. But what about the other areas? Circle the best answers below:

How often do I show respect to my children?

Never. Almost Never. Sometimes. Almost Always. Always.

How about flexibility? Do I take advantage of the teachable moments that come my way?

Never. Almost Never. Sometimes. Almost Always. Always.

If you circled *Always* for both, go to the head of the class! If not, spend some time together talking through a game plan on improvement in these areas.

When you get this plan into action, reward each other with "The Wisdom of Mrs. Green Award."

Last, But Not Least

It could have been a Norman Rockwell painting.

It was our local park. The baseball diamond was the key attraction, as little boys from all over the neighborhood met for a friendly game of nine innings. The kids were typical. Dirty faces, blue jeans with patched knees, T-shirts advertising a variety of products, and their most prized possession—their baseball gloves.

Yes, the scene was quite heartwarming. The two "best" baseball players became the captains. (It's interesting that no one chose the captains, they just assumed their authority from previous experience.) The two boys began choosing their teams. The picking order was pretty predictable . . . the choices went in order of skill in baseball, which was remarkably similar to the order in most other games.

As I watched this scene of Americana taking place, I suddenly felt a sharp pain in the depth of my stomach. I observed a little guy I hadn't seen before. This kid was strangely familiar, but it was like another time in history. Then it hit me. I realized who I was seeing.

The little kid was me.

Actually, I wasn't little. I was heavier than the other kids and nobody wanted a fat boy on their baseball team. I was back in my childhood, desperately desiring to play well, so I could be chosen quickly. But my neighborhood peers didn't think of me as a winning player, so I was constantly overlooked in the choosing.

How can you overlook a kid as fat as me? I thought to myself cynically. I didn't say a word, but my eyes grew wider with each choice. The expression on my face silently pleaded with each captain to choose me. Soon, though, the inevitable came.

"Okay," barked the captain of the first team to his counterpart. "You've got Billy."

"I didn't pick him," he replied.
"You *have* to pick him, 'cause I had last pick."
"I don't want him . . . he's too fat."
"You've gotta take him . . . use him as backstop."
"Oh, all right, if I have to. Come on, Butterball, just stay out of the way."

The damage was done. The message was loud and clear. I'm not good enough and they don't want me.

It's the curse of being picked last. It was ridicule, childish, but devastating. It was the pain of peers pressuring me to perform in a way I couldn't.

It was rejection.

Those blasted neighborhood "winners" constantly plotted out games, contests, quizzes, and rating scales that left "losers" like me no other choice but reluctant participation.

I concluded the pain of humiliation was less than the pain of rejection.

If I ever managed to hit the baseball, oh, how they laughed as I attempted to run the bases. It was humiliating, but it was an important discovery.

I learned that everybody loves to laugh at a guy who willingly belittles himself. The laughter becomes acceptance and acceptance is the pinnacle of success to the neighborhood fat kid. The lesson was clear.

It's better to be laughed at than left out.

So for me it was comedy for companionship.

"I'll run the bases like a crazy man—if you'll let me play."

"I'll sing like a fat lady in the opera—if you'll let me play."

"I'll jump in the swimming pool with all my clothes on—if you'll let me play."

" . . . if you'll let me play . . . if you'll let me play."

My mind began to return to the present tense. I rubbed my eyes in an attempt to come back to the here and now.

That's all in the past, I think to myself. But the past is profound.

The sides are just about all picked. I see a little guy who appears thinner and weaker than the others. But he's a performer. He's got them laughing already. Even though everyone else is chosen, he's yelling out his motto . . .

"Last, but not least."

LL

Love keeps the last from being least.

Making It Stick

Psychologists have a word describing a method of overcoming the pain of last place. The word is *compensation*. This means that if a child is too heavy to run the bases, maybe he has the interest and talent to play a mean trumpet. Or if music isn't his bag, maybe he is inclined toward the most beautiful and productive vegetable garden on the block. Or maybe he is a writer, mathematician, or chemist. If he can't swing a bat, perhaps he can kick a ball of another shape.

Every one of your children is good at something. Do you know what it is? Sit down with your mate and talk about it. Ask yourselves additional questions like: What are we doing to underscore the importance of these areas of competency? How are we balancing out the reality of weaknesses with the ecstasy of strength? How are we contributing to the establishment of a healthy self-image in our children?

Don't overlook compensation. Your child wanted me to tell you, because he/she felt uncomfortable having to bring it up. Go for it, Mom and Dad.

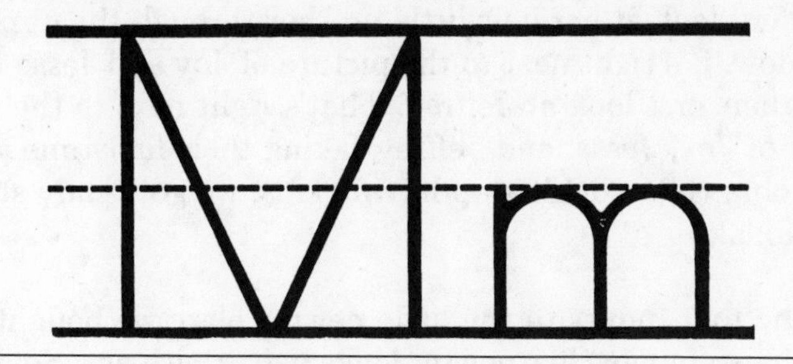

Museum of Memories

Could you describe your house or apartment in one word? Where do you find yourself in the spectrum that runs from "priceless, one-of-a-kind antiques" to the other extreme of "early K-Mart and Parisian particle board"? Let me tell you about my place.

I live in a museum.

Are you impressed? Maybe I should explain. Our home is far from perfect. If my house were meticulously decorated, I'd feel terribly uncomfortable sitting around in my shorts. Cozy and comfortable, that's our place. Not a dump, not a showplace—a home.

But it is also a museum . . . a museum of memories.

A favorite pastime of mine is to sit in our living room, late at night after everyone's asleep. While I'm relaxing there, I take a visual tour through our museum.

Our first stop is the picture of Joy and me. She's taking her first look at her new little brother through the nursery window. It's right next to the picture of Joy and Jesse taking their first look at Jeffrey. That's right next to the picture of Joy, Jesse, and Jeffrey taking their first-time gaze at John. (If we don't stop having kids, we gotta buy stock in Kodak.)

The tour moves to the little pewter plate we bought on our honeymoon. Gee, pewter looks better with age. So does my wife.

Over on the hutch in the dining room, I observe a chorus of bells. I pick one up for Rhonda every time I'm out of town overnight. Come to think of it, I've never seen a bell from New Mexico on anyone else's hutch. Pretty unique.

How about that shot of Jesse hugging Donald Duck! You know what's so good about it? It was spontaneous. I tried for hours to pose a shot, but those other kids kept getting in the way, and they didn't speak English. I'm glad my finger wasn't over the lens.

Step over here folks and you'll see our next exhibit. It's a plaque we were given from the Sunday school class we were in before we moved to California. We'll never forget some of those young married couples who still pray for us today.

Look at that coffee table. Haven't the kids been great about antiquing it? It sure has the look of real age . . . nicks, dings, splits, maybe even a water stain from Abe Lincoln's water glass! It's a fun piece of furniture. Joy put a blanket over it and made it into a playhouse. Jesse used to "preach" on top of it. Jeffrey set a world's record on it for the greatest number of Matchbox trucks on a tabletop. John teethes on it. And, of course, I stub my toe on it.

Our wooden rocking chair. I remember we bought it so we could rock our first baby. We had a good time too. The chair kind of "walks" as you rock in it. One night Rhonda rocked the baby so long that by the time he was asleep, she was in the laundry room.

Gather around this area and you'll see a picture of our first date. Here's one a year later, holding hands (slow starter, but great in the gun lap). And you'll notice a picture of our family every year since. I'm wearing the same sportcoat in the first few shots, but once we got married the blazer experienced incredible shrinkage. Rhonda is really big on pictures. Sure, I gripe, but it's those quiet tours of our museum that cause me to thank the Lord for her faithful persistence.

I'm also glad I didn't wait years before taking this tour. Sometimes it's left to the year the last child moves out. That's too late for me. My museum is still in its building process. There will be some major additions in years to come, and that's okay with me. I want to do all I can to be a part of them.

Well, I get a little misty-eyed when I take this museum tour. I didn't even get to the clock, Rhonda's needlework, the red plate, the macrame, or the Mrs. Butterworth's syrup bottle.

Maybe you can visit your museum real soon. It's something just for you. And just for old time's sake, on your way out, find the coffee table and stub your toe.

Mm

Make a tour of your Museum of Memories. It's a great field trip.

Making It Stick

I can think of several fun projects that could evolve out of this concept of Museums of Memories. Here are a few suggestions:

Write out your own Museum of Memories as individual family members. (Maybe Mom and Dad are the only ones old enough to write this out, but don't be too quick to overlook young ones who may want to "talk through" their own museums.) After you've finished, take the rest of your family through your museum. It'll be fun to see what items have special significance to some family members, while other items are important to everyone.

Another idea is to work together as a family on a Family Museum of Memories—with contributions from every family member. Perhaps you'd like to invite another family of friends over to take the tour of your museum.

One last possibility is to "go all out" on a real tour of your Museum of Memories. Dress up in an outfit that resembles a tour guide's, pass out tickets, meet the family at the front door, take them on your carefully prepared tour, and end up with a surprise picnic lunch on the museum grounds!

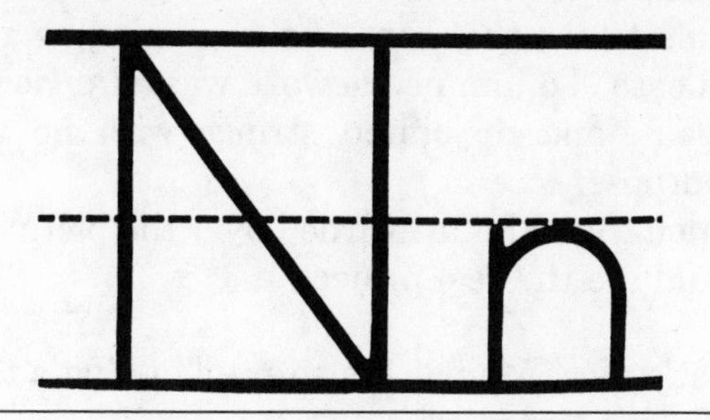

Needlework of God

Kids are great teachers.

This happened a while ago, but the lesson has lingered.

My wife finds great enjoyment and fulfillment in needlework. She's most content curled up in a cozy chair, creating with crewel or counted cross-stitch.

One night, as Rhonda was working on her project, I overheard Jeffrey contribute his own editorial comment on Mama's craft.

"Mama, that pitcher looks yukky!"

I thought that was a pretty harsh critique coming from the mouth of a two-year-old. I looked up at him, ready to reprove him when I noticed his perspective on the issue.

He was staring at the back of the needlework.

Living life down there among the two-year-olds, Jeffrey was not able to see the front of the picture, as any adult could with ease. To him needlework was a tangle of knots, loose threads, and disjointed strings with no apparent order or purpose.

It was then that Rhonda turned over the picture so that Jeffrey could see the real project.

"Oh, that's nice, Mama! It's so pity!" (That's two-year-old talk for "it's so pretty!")

Once he saw it from the right perspective, it became beautiful in his little eyes.

Many of us are faced with similar circumstances in our Christian lives. God has put us through some things that can best be described by the word *yukky*.

As we look at these times of trial in our lives, it's easy to take the child's perspective. Life can look pretty tangled and disjointed from the human side.

But remember, we are God's handiwork.

He is creating within us a beautiful needlework. During the time of endurance, it's important to remember that the result is greater resemblance to His character.

For there will come a point in time when God will turn over His needlework in order for us to see the beauty, order, and purpose to His work in our lives.

It's a whole different picture from God's perspective.

Just as kids don't always understand the adult perspective, humans don't always understand the work of God.

Non-Christians find it especially difficult to comprehend

why God would allow difficulty to enter our lives. They don't understand the process of purifying. They don't know of the Refiner's fire.

But remember, fellow Christians, it is all for our good. Don't allow the doubter to discourage you.

The doubter says your life is "PITY" and he means it literally.

But you and I know that your life is "PITY," which is the opposite of "YUKKY."

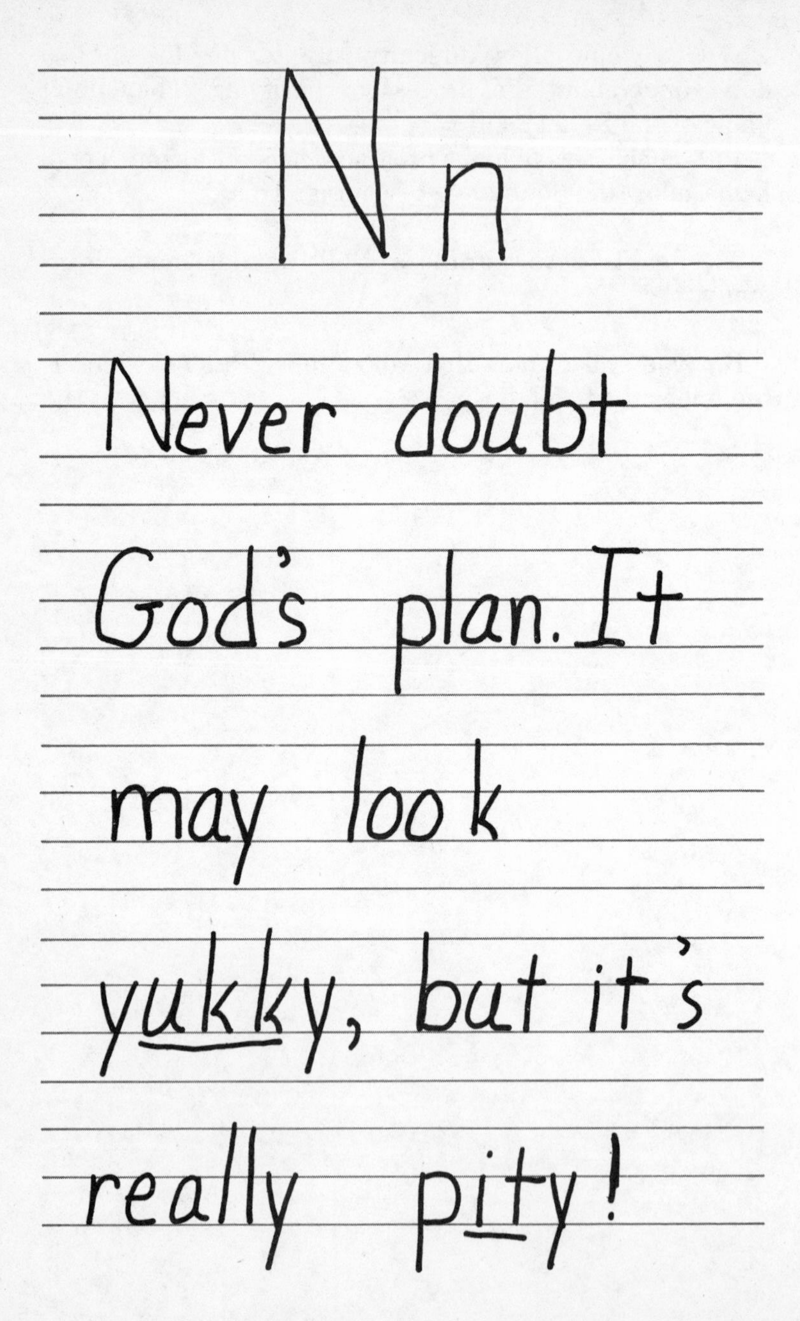
Nn
Never doubt
God's plan. It
may look
yukky, but it's
really pity!

Making It Stick

Every parent has the tendency to shelter his child from the tough times in life. As adults, we feel a need to insulate a child from YUKKINESS. If it's not PITY, it's not for my kids.

So let's pause for a few moments and think through this issue. Does my child know about God's master plan? Does he or she realize it may include the rough spots in life?

How am I helping my child prepare for the crunchy days of life ahead?

Next time you see one of those teachable moments, tell your kids the story of Job from the Old Testament. Be ready for questions like "Was that fair?" "Would God do that to me?" "What would you do in that yukky time, Mommy and Daddy?"

Finish up by telling the story of Jeffrey and the needlework. Let them realize that God has another side to our lives in which all things work together for beautiful artwork. It's PITY!

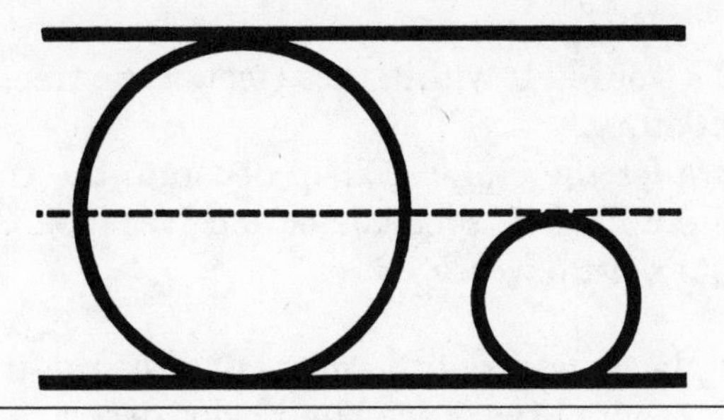

One Messy Christmas Tree

Have you ever stopped and studied one of those Christmas cards you've sent out? You know the ones—the front of the card is a Currier and Ives print of "Christmas in the Drawing Room." The room is decorated with impeccable taste, the fire is glowing, snow is falling on the other side of the window. The boughs of holly are decked through the adjoining halls. Mistletoe is carefully hung in discreet sections of the room.

And, of course, there's the Christmas Tree.

It is perfect. A delicate blend of tinsel, ribbons, bows, balls, toy soldiers, candles, bells, sugarplums, candy canes, all capped off with the silver star aboard the highest bough.

Yes, whenever I observe a setting of this nature, I lean back in my chair and make one heartwarming conclusion . . .

Currier and Ives must have been confirmed bachelors.

If you let your kids within three feet of the tree, it's quite a different story.

Since we let the children help decorate the tree, we've never quite pulled off the Currier and Ives look. And each year it gets a little worse!

At our place we make the decorating of the tree a real important family time. Each child helps decorate by hanging ornaments on the tree. The ornaments are all of special significance so we take time to explain each one. We have little styrofoam angels that the older kids made when they were preschoolers. We have hand-painted ornaments given to us by friends. We have engraved gold ornaments from relatives. We even have ornaments of our own design from years gone by.

When the kids hang the stuff, obviously they cover the lower portion of the tree. When that area is filled, Mama and Dad take over and fill in the upper part.

Are you getting the picture? The upper portion of the tree is decorated by two adults and the lower portion is attacked by four little ones!

That's right, a schizophrenic Christmas tree.

You know what we've noticed? The messy portion keeps getting bigger each year. As the kids grow, they take on more and more of the tree.

Sometimes as I sit by the tree, late at night, in those reflective moments, I think back to when the kids' portion of the tree was just a branch or two. I get a little misty as I realize just how fast time is going. Before you know, they'll be tall enough to do it all . . . even the star. I'll be looking up to them!

Just as I'm tempted to shudder at the thought of an entire tree decorated by the children, an even more sobering thought crosses my mind:

Before I know it, the entire tree will be decorated by two adults.

It's then that I realize how fortunate I am to have a messy tree. As a matter of fact, a messy tree is one of God's greatest gifts to me.

So, if you're ever visiting our house during the Christmas season, don't be looking for a modern-day version of Currier and Ives. Instead, come looking for a lovely testimony to Christmas at the Butterworth home . . .

. . . one Messy Christmas Tree.

Oo

Our messiness is often our most meaningful memory.

Making It Stick

Lots of parents are experts on the subject "What my children do to get on my nerves." We could fire out answers with incredible rapidity.

Here's a curve ball, Mom and Dad. What do your children do that you will miss when they are gone? That sort of question could radically change your approach to parenting!

Remember, your job as parent is temporary. Before you realize it, the kids are grown and gone.

What will you miss when they're gone? That's a good topic for discussion on a cold night by a warm fire, or on a warm night out on the porch swing. It's the kind of question that brings PERSPECTIVE. We realize our humanness, our limitations, our priorities, our shortcomings, and our needs.

So, if you haven't asked yourself this question in a while, do so. However if you have had this discussion recently, just go on from there. Thinking about this issue *too much* can create a deeper problem than the original subject at hand!

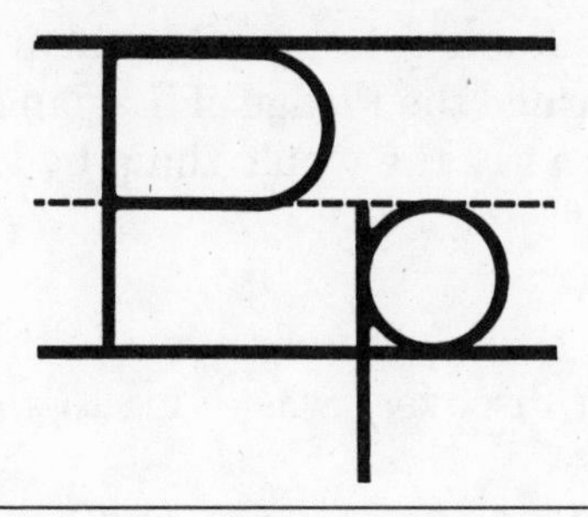

Pledge 'Legiance

The delight of discovery is exhilarating.

It's an unparalleled feeling of freshness. You may find something you never before found. You may stumble onto a nugget of truth that gives new hope in life's climb. Or you may learn something that you've seen in others' lives, but never personally possessed.

Our little Joy Lynn came home from her kindergarten class one day with a smile bigger than her cute little face could contain.

"Daddy, Daddy, guess what we learned in school today?"

"Gee, sweetie, I don't know," I replied. "But I bet you sure would like to tell me!"

"You're right, Daddy," she continued to blurt out her words in record speed, emphasizing her excitement.

"Well, come on, tell me. Don't keep me in suspense any longer!" I pleaded, much to her enjoyment.

"Today we learned the Pledge of 'Legiance!" she beamed with pride. "I can say the whole thing by heart . . . I don't even need a flag!"

I could tell by the look in her eye and the expression on her face that her discovery was dying to get out.

"Would you like to recite it for me?" I asked.

That innocent little question was received with the same enthusiasm you get with questions like: "Who wants a new box of crayons?" or, "Would you like to go to the park?" or, "Mama's out for the evening; who wants donuts for dinner?"

"Oh, Daddy, I'd *love* to. I'll stand up and say the whole thing without no help!"

"Any help," I corrected.

"No, really, I can do it," she responded, missing my point.

"Here goes." She cleared her throat, stood up straight and tall, and began to demonstrate her discovery.

I pledge 'legiance to the flag,
Of the 'Nited States of 'Merica.
And to the 'Public for whichit stans,
One Nation, under God, innavisible.
With liberty and justice for all.
Please be seated.

She sat down.

"Wow!" I shouted. "that's great . . . please say it again!" And so she did. And just as I suspected, it once again included the line, "Please be seated."

So there was a little kindergartener who thought the Pledge of Allegiance is one line longer than everyone else thinks it is. But there's something more.

This underscored to me that there's a big difference between rote memory and real meaning.

Education experts tell us the lowest level of learning is rote memory. The reason for that is because you can memorize, yet totally bypass understanding.

Christians of all ages run a similar risk. They can quote their pledge from their Book, yet avoid any personal penetration. We can master the lingo, the jargon, the answers, the posture, but send application on permanent vacation.

Well, Joy is older now. She's shortened her version of the pledge. She's even getting a better idea of its meaning. Her Christianity is coming along, too.

How's *your* Christianity? A recitation? Or a reality?

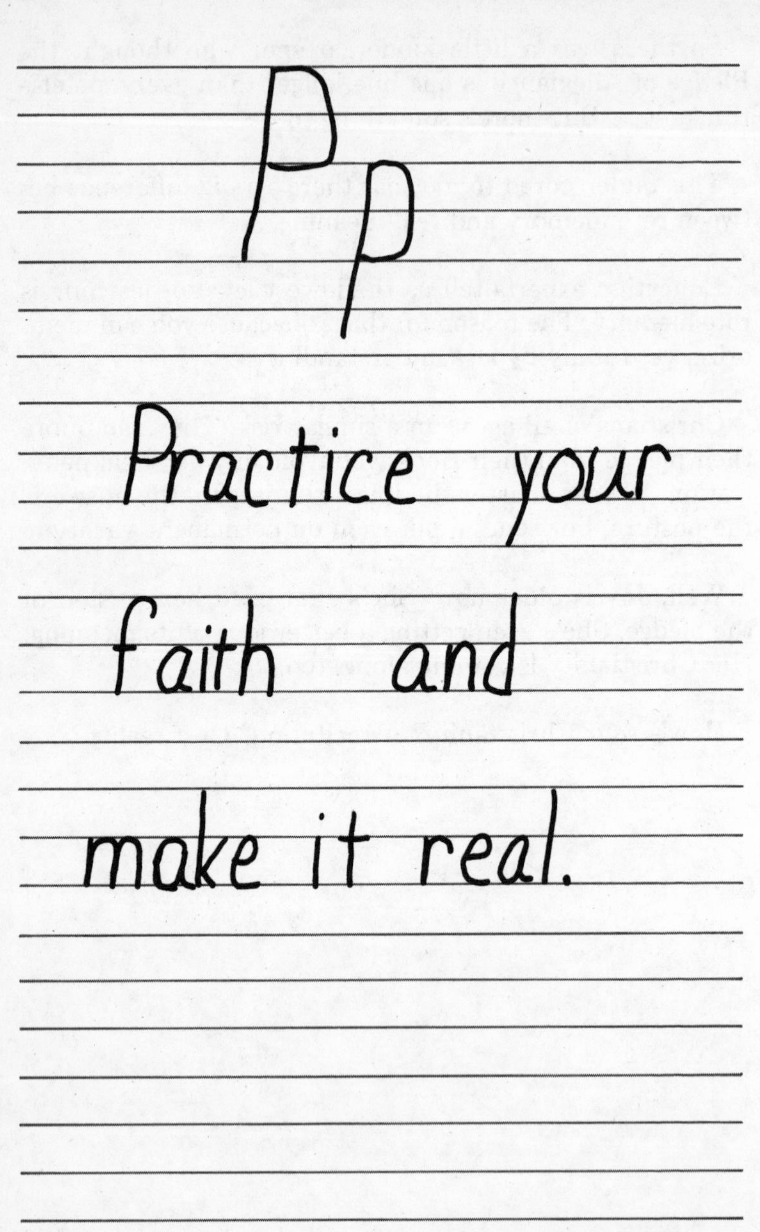
Pp
Practice your
faith and
make it real.

Making It Stick

If your children are old enough to read the story of Joy and her version of the Pledge, have them read it. If they're too young, tell them the story and explain the difference between reality and reciting.

Ask them if they view the values you are attempting to teach them as REAL or just something they RECITE.

This discussion could be quite revealing. As moms and dads, sometimes we want to believe in our kids so much, that we don't see some of the "roles" they're playing on our behalf.

One more suggestion: If your kids don't give you the answers you had hoped to hear, don't get angry. Remember . . . you asked for it. Set a goal to discuss the issue in order to reach a plan for translating roles into reality.

You'll be grateful you did.

Your kids will be grateful forever.

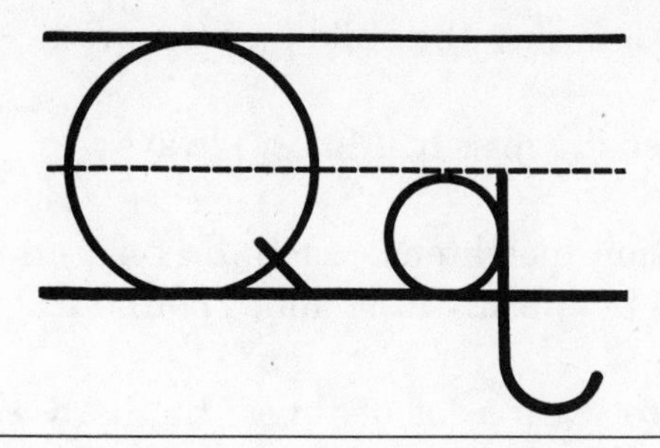

Quick to Hear

You can fool some of the people all of the time, and all of the people some of the time. . . .

I've tried on numerous occasions to convince the kids that I've been paying attention when I've really been daydreaming. It's a losing battle. They've got me figured out.

The classic illustration occurs when we're out driving. We have one of those big nine-passenger station wagons, so we usually sit in the following order: Joy and Jesse are buckled into the very backseat, Jeffrey and John are strapped into their car seats situated in the middle of the car, and Mom and Dad are strategically located in the front.

As we are driving down the road, one of the kids will suddenly shriek, "WOW, LOOK AT THAT EVERY-

BODY!!!" Of course, we are all supposed to know in advance what it is that the child has observed.

But we usually miss it. Almost always.

The tension heightens when driving on a freeway. Things pass by quickly at 55 miles per hour.

I've had to learn a lot of things the hard way. When I would honestly admit to not seeing what the child saw, I was slapped with charges of being uninterested, uninvolved, apathetic, dull of wits.

Since I didn't want my children to grow up with a father of such bad reputation, I had to improvise. So when we would pass points of interest and the kids would yell out their lines, I would immediately respond, *"Yeah!"* giving the impression that I, too, was equally impressed with the passing attraction.

They didn't buy that for a minute.

Ultimately it was Jeffrey who called me on it.

We were out driving and he saw something that excited him. He blurted out, "WOW!! EVERYBODY LOOK AT DAT!!!"

Right away I went into my routine. *"Yeah,"* I replied, acting interested and involved.

At this point I felt these two little hands reach over from the middle seat and firmly grasp my cheeks. Jeffrey knows that when we talk seriously, I hold his face firmly, so he won't be distracted. He obviously felt the same seriousness was appropriate for this conversation.

With my head firmly in his grasp, he passed down his indictment firmly and succinctly. He simply uttered, "Don't say, 'Yeah,' Dad. Don't say, 'Yeah.' "

Once again I had been found out.

Jeffrey realized that I could say "Yeah," simply out of reflex. When the audible sound waves from his voice concluded, I'd respond.

I *heard* him, but I didn't *listen* to him.

If I were listening, I would have had a chance to catch his excitement out of the corner of my eye and the corner of my rearview mirror. But I was too preoccupied with other things (not even driving, sad to say), so I was unable to give my son the attention he deserved.

So beware of the trap. We all know the weakness that accompanies a "Yes Man." Now you know the same applies to a "Yeah Man."

Kids hate hearers.

Kids love listeners.

Know what I mean?

Don't say, "Yeah."

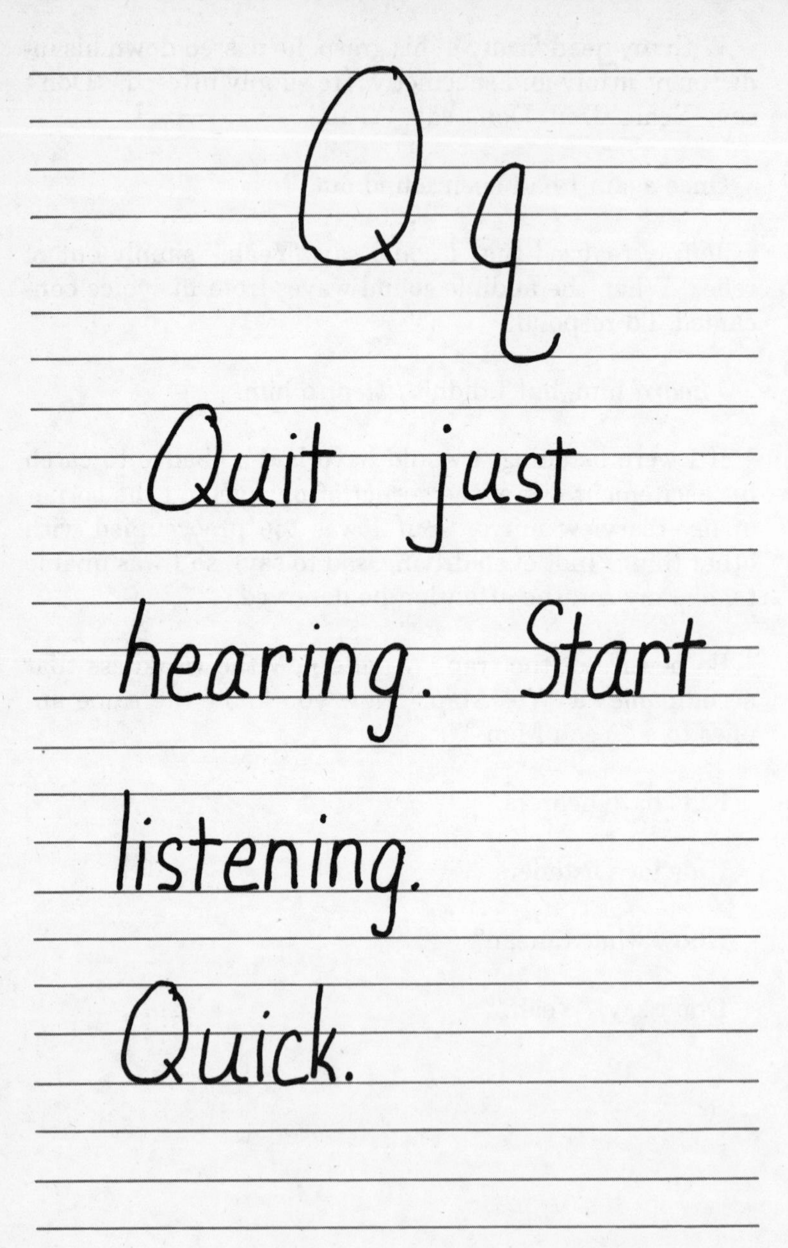
Q q
Quit just
hearing. Start
listening.
Quick.

Making It Stick

I wonder what God was trying to emphasize when He made man with one mouth and two ears. Sounds like a vote of confidence for quick hearers.

Quick hearers are good listeners. But good listening isn't developed overnight. It takes work—real concentration.

If you're a poor listener, try implementing this suggestion into your life. Become an ACTIVE LISTENER. Active listeners are people who give regular verbal feedback to those to whom they are listening. It's also called *paraphrasing*.

So if your mate or one of your children mentions something to you, as an active listener you will probably begin by saying: "What I hear you saying is . . . " and then rephrasing what you understood to be said. Continue with questions like, "How do you feel about this?" Get underneath the words to the real meaning.

Obviously this is more demanding than "passive listening" but the rewards are rich. You'll be achieving the ultimate goal in any form of communication . . .

. . . understanding.

Y'all try this now, hear!

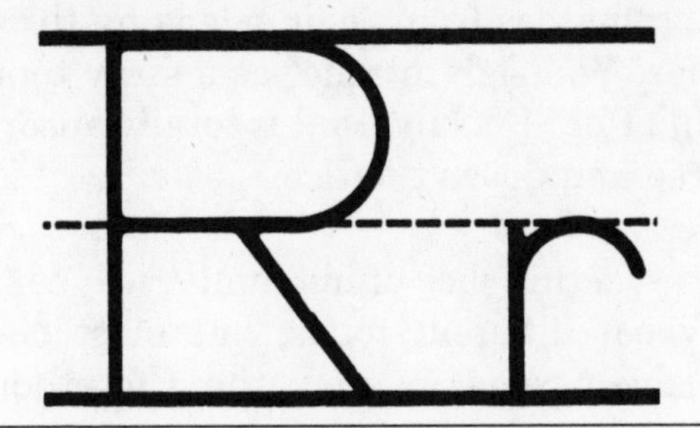

Remember: Slow to Speak

Next time you're really bored, take a field trip to the local cafeteria. Don't eat . . . just observe. It's a great visual aid on speaking without thinking.

First in line is Harry Girder, the steelworker and his tiny wife, Gert. Notice the first dish available. Right—dessert. Without even thinking, Harry asks for the chocolate cake. Gert impulsively requests the strawberry shortcake, vowing to give up potatoes.

Following Gert is Phil Preppy, who balances two trays in each hand. Phil is somewhat of a local hero at the cafeteria since he virtually moved in during the last spring break. He eats everything in sight, filling out his pink Izod quite nicely.

Behind Phil is Barb Big-Eyes who can't resist anything. Stick around though, she won't eat half the food on her tray.

Things are tense for a few moments when two little boys remove the tomatoes from their salads by throwing them at each other. You sigh in relief as a stray tomato misses Barb and hits Phil. Luckily, Phil is totally absorbed in tray number three and doesn't notice.

As we observe this slice of humanity, we see clearly that people may eat different foods, but most choose those foods impulsively, speaking up without forethought.

I get the biggest kick watching my own kids in this cafeteria setting. They have the same tendencies as Barb, Phil, Harry, and Gert. They want it all.

Well, since the kids are so impulsive, I decided that this would be an excellent setting in which to discuss the advantages of thinking before speaking. You know, pausing to think through the best choice, instead of just barking out the names of all the foods.

"Now before you ask the lady for a particular dish," I began, "think about it. Is this what you *really* want? Will you eat it up or just pick at it? Think about the best choice."

"But that takes all the fun out of it, Dad!" protested the kids chorus.

"Think first," I reviewed. "Be slow to speak."

They know I've got 'em when I quote Scripture.

But the lesson was learned . . . almost too well.

Yes, instead of impulsive idiocy, I got slow-motion agony.

They brainstormed over desserts; they calculated over

salads; they pondered over vegetables; they mused over meats.

Thinking before you speak is wiser, but it's also slower. And of course, a child's thought process is certainly a crash course in creative logic.

At the meats, for example, the choice was between steak (filet mignon, no less!) and half a baked chicken on a bed of rice. Unaware of the prices on any items, the kids huddled together and announced their choice.

"We'll take chicken."

"Great," I sighed, checking my wallet. "Tell me, why chicken over steak?" I was curious.

"That's easy, Dad," they smiled. "The steak is little, the chicken is big. That's why chicken is the best!" Then they added, "Aren't we good thinkers?"

"You sure are," I laughed.

They *were* thinking. That was the important thing. Sure, there will come the time when they realize size isn't the only difference between filet mignon and chicken . . .

. . . but by then, I'll have saved up enough money from their chicken meals to put them through college.

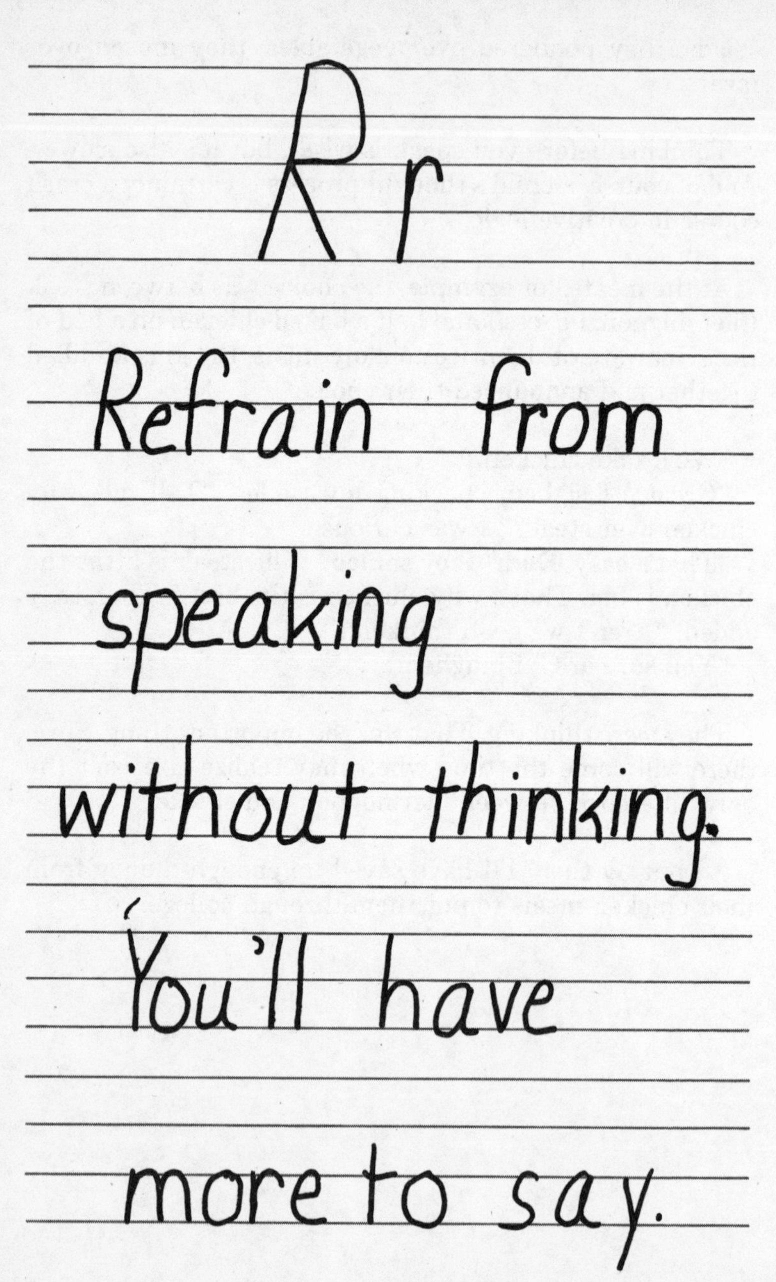
Rr
Refrain from
speaking
without thinking.
You'll have
more to say.

Making It Stick

Do you think before you speak?

Think about your answer before you give it to me. Some will answer, "Never." Some will answer, "Always." Most of us will answer, "Sometimes I do and sometimes I don't." Let's work on a plan to prevent the "sometimes I don't" in our lives.

The plan involves ACCOUNTABILITY. That means you need a friend or family member to whom you will be *accountable* for what you say. Meet with this person on a regular basis, at least once every two weeks if possible. Talk about the victories you experienced during the last few days. Tell about the temptations to speak abruptly, but how you kept yourself in check.

You'll also need to address the times when temptation arose and you yielded. Being fully accountable to this person means sharing the rough stuff, too. It's in this type of vulnerability that real progress is made.

It's a good idea.

Think about it.

Ss

Slow to Anger

I blew it.

Uncommon words from parents, yet a very common description of parenting. We moms and dads have this aversion to admitting our weaknesses . . . especially in front of the kids. The irony is the kids know our shortcomings better than anyone. But we still hold to the theory that states, "If I don't admit it, it's not noticeable."

I took Joy and Jesse with me to the grocery store the other day. They're both good kids, but they can slowly and systematically wear you down. You know the types of requests . . .

- "Can I push the cart?"
- "Can I get the tomato sauce?"
- "Can we have candy?"
- "Can I ride in the cart?"

- "How much more stuff do we need?"
- "Is there a bathroom in this store?"
- "Can I pick out the cereal?"
- "Why can't we eat the food NOW?"
- "Do we have to buy those vegetables?"
- "Can I help unload the cart?"
- "Can I give the lady the money?"
- "Can I help, please?"

Well, you would have been proud of me. I kept my composure through every aisle of the store, including checkout. We put the groceries in the back of the station wagon and headed home. Of course, the questions were still bombarding me in rapid succession . . .

- "Can I open the car door when we get home?"
- "Can I open the front door when we get home?"
- "Can I use the bathroom first?"
- "Can I give Mama her little surprise?"
- "Can I unbuckle my seat belt early?"
- "Can I sit in John's car seat?"
- "Can I hold your keys when we get home?"
- "Can I help you unload the groceries?"

This went on for the entire excursion. As a matter of fact, all I remember saying the entire trip was, "No, No, Yes, No, Yes, No, No, No, No, Yes, Yes, Soon, No, No, Over there, No, No, We'll see."

When we arrived home, I let the kids help me unload the groceries in the usual manner—I give them easy, unbreakable items to carry. But this particular trip they were not satisfied with diapers, dog food, and paper napkins. They wanted more.

"Please, Daddy, let me carry one more bag for you, please?"

It was Jesse, turning on the charm. "Look Daddy, here's a bag with paper towels in it. Can I carry this one in, please?"

I reluctantly agreed. I knew there had to be more in the bag than paper towels, but I couldn't recall what else. However, when Jesse allowed the bag to meet our concrete porch step at high speed, I soon saw what else the bag contained.

A glass jar of apple juice.

In order to try to make things better, Jesse took the remainder of the bag into the kitchen and began looking for a rag for some cleanup.

It only made things worse.

He transported apple juice to every floor in our house. That's right, now we had Sticky Apple Porch, Sticky Apple Carpet, Sticky Apple Hardwood Floor, and Sticky Apple Floor Tiles.

I snapped out—
"GET INTO YOUR ROOM, YOUNG MAN!!! YOU CAN'T DO ANYTHING RIGHT!!! I WILL NEVER, EVER, LET YOU HELP ME WITH THE GROCERIES AGAIN!!! YOU WILL NOT BE ALLOWED TO GO TO THE STORE WITH ME AGAIN, EITHER!!! GO TO YOUR ROOM, I'LL BE IN SHORTLY WITH THE PADDLE!!!"

To put this another way, everything you've ever read about proper parenting was violated in a statement of anger.

In an attempt to cool down, I tried to wipe up the floor with a Sticky Apple Mop. It only seemed to spread the stuff farther.

But it's during those moments when a parent is cooling down that he realizes how foolish it is to blow up. Here we had a precious little blond-haired gift from God reduced to the price of a jar of apple juice. It just wasn't right.

So, instead of marching into Jesse's room with a paddle, I crawled in with an apology.

He was still sobbing, terribly upset over what had happened. I picked him up, put him on my lap, and whispered, "Jesse, I'm so sorry I exploded and yelled. I really do love you. Please forgive me."

Those big blue eyes looked up at me and smiled. He immediately responded, "That's okay, Daddy. I love you, too."

Well, I couldn't control the emotion of the moment. So, of all the dumb things to do, I started to cry . . . I mean weep . . . sob . . . uncontrollably . . . like a baby.

We hugged and hugged and hugged and hugged.

After I promised Jesse that I would try not to blow up again, he just passed it off. "Don't worry about it, Dad. It's okay, I understand."

Then my little joker couldn't resist some fun. Through a blend of tears and smiles came this line: "Anyway, Dad, you know what? You sure do cry funny!!"

So I'm trying to blow up less and break down more.

'Cause to my kids, one is scary, but the other is funny.

Ss

Sinless parents don't exist.

Admit it.

Making It Stick

Anger that goes unchecked can be cancerous to a relationship. Dealing with the blowup is absolutely vital. I think that's why Paul encouraged the Ephesians " . . . Do not let the sun go down on your anger" (Ephesians 4:26).

So let's attempt to pinpoint some patterns in bouts with anger that you may have as a parent. Complete the following statements honestly. Answer the questions objectively. Then, see if there are habits or recurring events that trigger anger. The purpose of this project is to allow you to become familiar with your behavior patterns. Hopefully, if you can recognize circumstances that normally lead to anger, you can "head it off at the pass" by being prepared to deal with it.

- I most often get angry at (what time of day) ________________.

- I most often get angry at (which particular family member) ________________.

- After I "blow up" I usually feel ________________.

- My children see me "work through" my anger (always, sometimes, never) ________________.

- I apologize for "blowing it" (always, sometimes, never) ______________.

- How does God view my anger?

- How can He help me get a better handle on it?

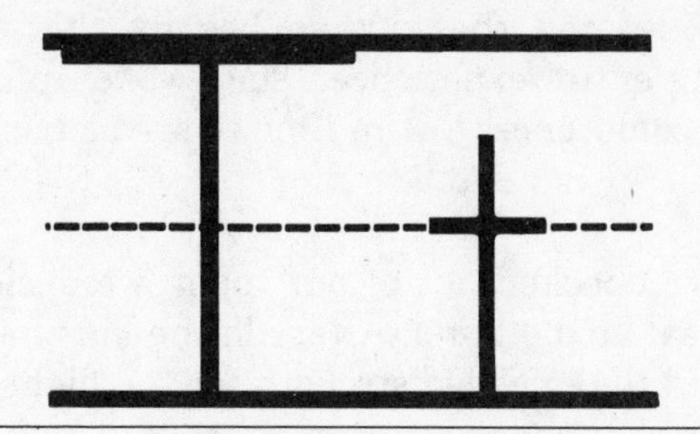

True Tales of Terror While Traveling

Taking an airline excursion with one wife, four kids, and enough luggage to keep thirty-seven gorillas hopping is no picnic. I'm sure it's no coincidence that one day after our return flight the airline went out of business. Several years ago I was foolish enough to agree to speak at a conference in the mountains of Tennessee on the weekend between Christmas and New Year's. Flying during a holiday weekend convinces me that all the houses we fly over have to be empty because all the people are either in a plane or on standby.

Of course there are no nonstop flights between my home and the mountains of Tennessee. There aren't even direct flights. We're going to have a change of planes and a layover in Atlanta.

I don't have Scripture to support this, but I believe when a person dies, they don't go directly to heaven or hell. They first go to Atlanta for a layover.

Well, we made it to Tennessee just fine. See, we flew all night. We sedated the kids so heavily that they slept through the entire experience. They woke up on the last day of the conference, just in time to see us packing to return home.

Before we checked out of our room, we decided to eat one last meal at the hotel. After all, the kids hadn't eaten for days and they needed strength for the flight home.

This was a real classy hotel . . . it really was. But it had one fatal flaw—the food.

Our meals tasted as if they were prepared in a cement mixer by a direct descendant of John Wilkes Booth.

It was bubonic plague on a bun.

We turned in our key, said good-bye to our new friends from the conference, and set out in our rented subcompact car for the Tennessee Mountain Airport.

To say the car was crowded would be a lie. It was worse than crowded. It was barbaric torture. The seats were full of luggage, since subcompacts don't have trunks, just ashtrays.

After we had driven long enough to insure that everyone was carsick, we pulled up to the Tennessee Mountain Airport which looked like a Burger King Restaurant, only smaller.

Our flight was declared "open seating," so we quickly walked to the plane and found two seats in Row 23, two seats in Row 25, one seat in row 28, and one seat in Row 29.

Rhonda grabbed the first two for herself and Jeffrey, I grabbed the next two for John and myself, and I sent Joy and Jesse off with a wing and a prayer.

They got the seats.

Well, we worked hard at getting everybody all buckled in. As soon as all four were strapped in tight, Rhonda and I buckled in. Even before we were off the ground, we heard—

"I gotta go to the bathroom, Dad." It was in stereo, coming from both Row 28 and Row 29.

"You'll have to wait," I barked back four rows. "We're taxiing."

"This is a plane, Dad, not a cab," said Jeffrey in total seriousness from two rows ahead.

"We can't wait, Dad."

"You'll have to wait, kids."

As we climbed to 33,000 feet I heard the kids say, "Dad, we didn't."

"Didn't what?" I quizzed.

"Didn't wait," they replied.

"You mean you . . ."

"YUP."

I turned around to see the frowning glares of four rows of passengers.

I threw up my hands in a 'What Could I Do?' type of way.

Finally the seat belt light went out. I quickly jumped up in order to attend to the business in Rows 28 and 29. But I wasn't fast enough. Everyone else was watching for that seat belt sign to die. So when it did, the aisles turned crowded.

I laboriously made my way to Joy and Jesse. I firmly clenched their wet little hands and we worked our way back to the lavatory.

One adult and two kids in an airplane lavatory is a real trick. Every time I bent over to help one of the kids, I would bump both head and tail on opposite sides of the rest room.

All the kids' clothes were packed, so there was nothing to do but wash them down a little bit and try to get them to smell like airline soap.

By the time I got Joy and Jess back in their seats and made my way up to my seat, Rhonda was holding John with her arms totally outstretched.

So I had to once again make my way to the john for John. After saying, "Excuse me," forty-six times, I finally arrived at the rear of the plane.

Our little jaunt to Atlanta continued in much the same vein. It looked like a circus. It sounded like a cheerleading clinic. It smelled like . . . well, it smelled. And it felt terrible.

Finally, we touched down. Rhonda and I looked at each other with that 'I've never been so glad to be back on earth' look. We were exhausted.

Since we had at least an hour layover and had to change planes, we deplaned.

The change in scenery was therapeutic. It was nice to make trips not to an airplane rest room, but to an *airport* rest room instead.

The food had destroyed the kids' systems so I ran *many* trips to the lavatory. I felt like I was jogging.

One of the other disadvantages about flying on the weekend between Christmas and New Year's is that you'll miss one or two National Football League play-off games.

This really hurt me. The Cowboys were playing. They were *my* team. I think Tom Landry wrote a book of the Bible. I was missing it. I've known men who have made suicide attempts over like circumstances.

But as I was making my fifth run to the airport rest room, I observed a real find . . . airport rent-a-TVs. Dozens of little TVs that work at the sound of a quarter. Twenty-five cents for fifteen minutes.

I found an un-used set, popped in my quarter, and watched twenty-two grown men, all over two hundred pounds, appear on a screen that was five inches square.

The picture was so small, I never did see a football.

I kept mumbling for Pat Summerall or Gary Bender or John Madden to give the score, but they weren't listening.

The Cowboys got the ball and were in a hurry-up offense. The play was a long pass—bomb to the end zone. It looked like it was going to be a beauty. My heart raced as I sat on the edge of my seat. Would it be a score?

Suddenly, without warning, the TV turned off.

"Hey!" I yelled. "This thing's only been on three minutes! I paid for fifteen!"

No one was listening.

I fumbled around and found another quarter. By the time the TV turned on again, it was a commercial for Pepto-Bismol.

It was really appealing.

The game returned, but no mention of the score. I had to keep running kids to the rest room and I assumed they gave the score every time I left.

No one else would even tell me the score. They were so absorbed with their own five-square-inch world, they didn't even hear me ask.

I kept feeding that baby quarters every three minutes. So one hour later I was broke.

We returned to our gate for the next leg of our journey. (I never did find out the score until the next day back home!)

The journey from Atlanta to Los Angeles, though four times as long, went four times smoother than our first jaunt. There were three reasons why it was smooth:

- Everything the kids had ever eaten was past history. So, they put up their feet and slept for the entire flight.
- They were worn out from all those laps to the bathroom.
- I paid the pilot an extra twenty-five dollars to keep the seat belt light on for the entire flight.

The kids never moved.

Tt

Travel smart.

Plan ahead.

Making It Stick

What's your tale of traveling terror? Let's face it, we all have them.

But you know, as gruesome as this was for me, it was no picnic for the kids, either. And it was *my* idea, not theirs!

What can you do to make family travel more enjoyable? PLANNING is probably the key issue. Rhonda is great at this part of life. How carefully do you think through your times away as a family unit?

Sure, there are unexpected issues that will assault you during your trip, but there are aspects you can *anticipate* and in doing so, help yourself to a better trip.

So the answer to bad travel isn't to stop traveling! Travel makes memories for you and the kids. Don't cancel out this valuable dimension of family fun. Instead, just be a little more thorough in your preparations. Ask each other lots of questions. I've got one for you . . .

. . . What do you do with your kids while you're laid over in Atlanta?

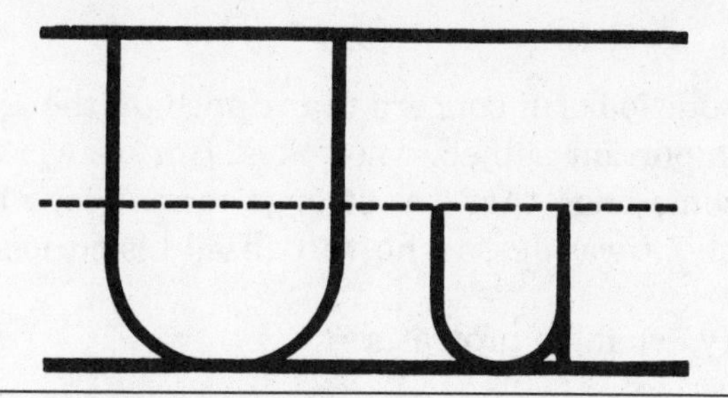

Uncomfortably Yours

Mealtimes are great family times. In some homes, it's the only guaranteed time of the day for the entire crew to gather together. Although the primary function of sitting around the table is eating, one of the nicest by-products is good, stimulating, family conversation. You can cover a lot of ground, if you know how to do it! You can talk about the office, school, home, church, the neighborhood, friends, relationships, and just about anything that would classify as current events.

Including some uncomfortable subjects.

The other day we were all in our seats at the table. We had just finished discussing the price of GI Joe Men in relation to weekly allowance and Rhonda was relating a news story she had read in the paper. It seems that a nationally known sports hero had been arrested for soliciting a prostitute. Rhonda and I both had that look of concern on our faces. We hate to hear of heroes falling from their pedestals.

It was our looks of concern that tipped off the kids. This was an important subject—no jokes. But we were tossing around some lingo that was strange terminology to them. Ultimately, it was Jesse who verbalized his curiosity.

"Daddy, what's a protsatute?"

I nervously glanced over at Rhonda. She gave me the same look of discomfort.

It's those few seconds right after the question that are the key. Oftentimes, it's simply a passing probing that is forgotten fast. But, other times, it's a real issue—in need of addressing.

Joy Lynn sealed our doom.

"Yeah, Dad, what is a prossatude?" she asked innocently.

We were stuck. No turning back now. It was time to deal with one of life's uncomfortable subjects. The catch was to communicate it on the level of a little one.

I cleared my throat and began by asking a rhetorical question, in order to buy some time.

"Do *any* of you know what a prostitute is?"

To my astonishment, little Jeffrey put up his hand as if it was an addition question in math class.

"Jeffrey, do you know what a prostitute is?" I quizzed.
"Yes," he responded. "Rae [an adult friend of ours] told me what they are!"

I sighed a sigh of deeper consternation and some relief. Who knows what Jeffrey may have understood as an answer? But there was hope he may have it right, thus sparing me the dilemma of definition.

"Okay, Jeff, tell us . . . what's a prostitute?"

"Well, let's see," Jeffrey began. I could tell by his opening remark, he *didn't* know, but felt compelled to offer a creative answer anyway.

Finally, he blurted out, "A prosletute is someone who speeds when they're driving!"

Rhonda suddenly began to cough. Apparently she had a morsel of food caught in her throat. In order to be polite, she turned her head away from the table.

"That's a good answer, Jeffrey," I encouraged, "but it's not right."

So the moment of truth arrived. *Here goes*, I thought to myself.

"You kids know how we call certain parts of your body 'private parts,' right?"

"Yeah," they responded.

"And no one is allowed to touch your private parts, right?"

"Right."

"Well, a prostitute is someone who lets other people touch her private parts in a certain way."

"Why do they let people do that, Daddy?" Joy asked.

"It's a very wrong thing to do," I continued, "But they do it 'cause people pay them money."

All four of them sat in awe. They never heard anything like that before, so I guess it was slow in sinking in. Just when I thought they were getting it, Jesse broke the silence.

"How much money do they get, Dad?"

I could see his little mind working. Based on our earlier topic of conversation, he wanted to translate the price into GI Joe Men.

"That's not the point, Jesse. The point is it's wrong to do—okay?"

"Okay," he said with a shrug of his shoulders. That was it, short and sweet, we then passed on to the next subject . . . why skateboards are outdoor toys.

But that night, as Rhonda and I talked before bed, we both agreed on the value of our mealtime message. It was uncomfortable—I was sweating—but very necessary. The times in which we live demand that we address these issues.

What are the uncomfortable subjects in your home? Are you using good judgment in your choice of words and choice of timing?

Beware of the excuse, "I'll wait till they're older." That can be roughly translated, "Someone else can tell them."

No—make those moments uncomfortably *yours*.

Uu

Understanding is the goal, both of the comfortable and the uncomfortable.

Making It Stick

What's the uncomfortable subject in your home?

Come on, now, don't shrug your shoulders at me. We both know you have at least one subject you've been avoiding with the children. Let's work through a strategy to deal with it the next occasion the timing is right.

Notice what I'm saying. I'm not suggesting you bring this subject up tomorrow night at dinner. But I am suggesting that you and your mate be prepared for the next time *the children* bring it up.

As you're hammering out your strategy, be sure to address the following issues:

- How can I deal with this issue directly, yet discreetly?
- How can I present it in terms they will be sure to understand?
- How much or how little should be said at this point in their lives?
- Is this a job for Dad only, Mom only, or a team presentation?
- Should all the kids be present or just the child with the question?
- Do we have enough towels handy to deal with the sweaty face and palms that usually accompany discussions of this nature?

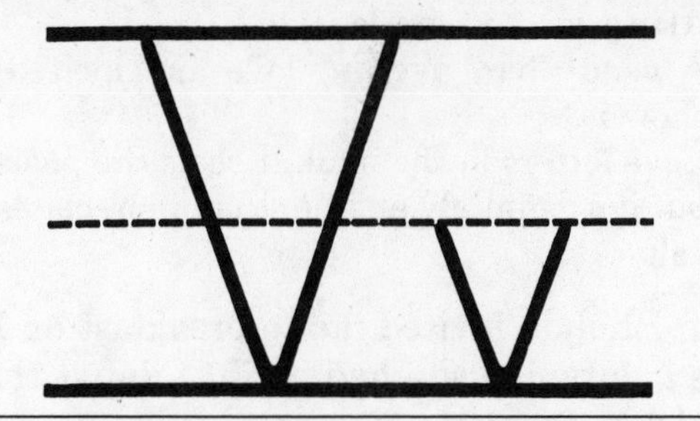

Very Important Present

We're big on gifts around our house.

Not just for birthdays or Christmas, either. We're a family that loves the godliness of giving, coupled with the humanness of loving to get! So it can be June 30 or March 7 or the nineteenth of October, it doesn't matter. We just love gifts.

Since we give a lot, we're not talking about new cars, washer/dryers, or Cabbage Patch Dolls. No, it's little, inexpensive stuff with great thought and meaning as its wrappings.

Stuff like:

- Pencil holders made out of frozen lemonade cans.
- Greeting cards cut out of old magazine pictures and print.

- Bookends made from old two-by-four scraps.
- Artwork—first-grade style.
- A candy bar given in love and melted to show it.
- Love letters in the mail. It costs the postage but it's definitely an item that appreciates in value.

So, when Rhonda invited me to breakfast on December 21 and she mentioned she had a gift, I didn't think it was anything highly unusual.

But it was.

I just figured it was an early Christmas gift. My wife is known to get excited about presents, so when she told me she couldn't wait till Christmas, I thought, *No big deal.*

I was wrong.

When we arrived at the restaurant, I casually ordered two breakfast specials—one bacon and eggs, eggs up, and wheat toast; and one ham and eggs, eggs scrambled, and sourdough toast—and yes, two coffees.

Rhonda, being a sly fox, reached into her purse in order to lead me to believe she had the gift inside. I concluded it was a nice card or another type of thoughtful gesture, but nothing really life-changing.

Little did I know.

Life is wild, spontaneous, and exhilarating at our place, but like I said, gifts are kind of a commonplace event. I didn't think gifts could necessarily fall under the category "exhilarating."

Wrong again.

As she fumbled around in her purse, I began to wonder just what it was that could be so hard to find in her tiny little clutch. She finally took her hand out and sighed, "The gift isn't in there, so I guess I'll just have to tell you what it is."

I surmised that this gift was home on the kitchen counter, or in the bedroom on a nightstand, or in the glove compartment, or at the baby-sitter's, or in another purse.

Wrong, wrong, wrong.

Suddenly Rhonda got one big smile on her face. A smile the likes of which I have only seen on a few other occasions. That smile should have been my tip-off, but I still was slow in picking up the plot.

Yes, all wise women throughout the world now know the gift. In search of my dignity, however, I still believe there are at least a few guys out there that haven't caught on. Like me, they operate on straightforwardness, not on implication.

Well, guys, two words cleared up the question about the gift. It made me so happy I cried right there in the restaurant. If you've been there, you know what I mean. The little woman looked at me and said,

"I'm pregnant."

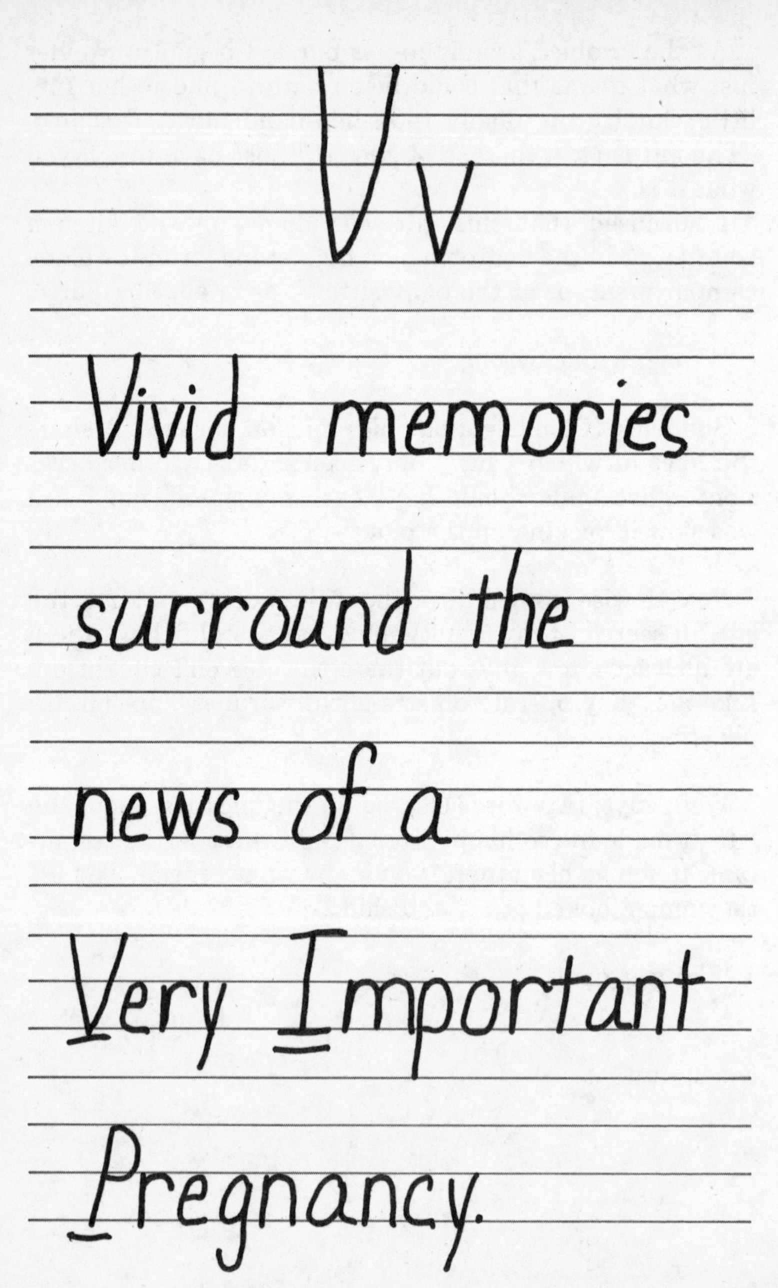
Vv
Vivid memories
surround the
news of a
Very Important
Pregnancy.

Making It Stick

Well, all the moms are sighing and all the dads are groaning! But hold on, you should've guessed by now that the only thing better than four little Butters is . . . five little Butters!

Do you remember the circumstances surrounding your pregnancy discoveries? That's an easy question for some, difficult for others. Well, not only do I want you two to discuss that question, but I'm prepared with an arsenal of questions for our own version of "Parental Trivia." I suggest that the person who answers the most questions correctly gets to pick the restaurant for your next "date."

We'll start out easy and work up to the tough ones:

- Describe your first date.
- Describe how marriage was proposed.
- Name all the people in your wedding party. (Let's get tougher.)
- Describe the THIRD day of your honeymoon.
- What is the name of the hospital where you delivered your first child?
- If your first child was a boy, what were you going to name him if he had turned out to be a girl or vice versa?
- What did you do for your second child on his/her second birthday?

(One last one, just to get the guys back on my side.)

- What place in the standings was your favorite football, basketball, or baseball team, on the day your first child was born?

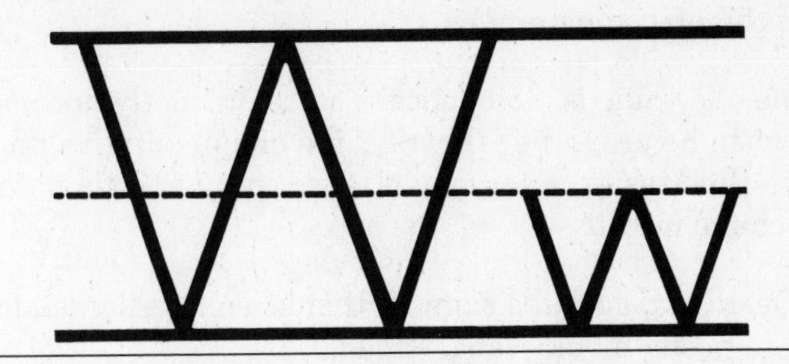

When Children Pray

Never close your eyes when you pray with four little kids.

Really, there's too much happening that you'll miss if you close your eyes. So, until you can get the kids to close their eyes, don't lose out on all the action.

Our youngest son, John, has brought new dimensions to our family's prayer life. He has a sincere, earnest desire to communicate with God, yet he is rather *unorthodox* in his approach.

I must confess, however, I find his approach rather refreshing.

We usually pray at the dinner table. We all find our places and proceed to hold hands for a family prayer of thanks. Sometimes I pray, sometimes Rhonda, sometimes one of the kids, sometimes a combination. John usually holds hands with Mama and Joy and mimics what he hears from the preceding prayer.

The odd thing is, John speaks quite distinctly normally, but when he prays, he jabbers. Kind of a meditative mumble to the Master. Everyone else will pray and then John will chime in with—

"Dear God, do waba sami ko thanks ooh goshaman laba food to posha mooky tana. Amen."

This is also a good example of why I pray with my eyes open. John whispers his prayer so softly, that I have to read his lips to see the magic word of wrap-up . . . "Amen."

The other evening while we were praying around the table, I happened to open my eyes to better hear one of Jeffrey's prayers. While my eyes were open, I chanced upon another important discovery.

Holding hands while praying promotes a oneness in the family. There's a special unity we can feel as we touch one another.

Pragmatically speaking, holding hands while praying before dinner also keeps little hands out of the food!

But John doesn't need his hands to eat.

As I opened my eyes to lip-read Jeffrey, I found John leaned over in his high chair, seemingly in an attitude of prayer, but in reality, eating his dinner like a dog.

That's right, face in the dish, lapping it up with his tongue, wearing it from hairline to neckline.

I couldn't believe it. I concluded John must have an incredible tongue, because he can lick his whole face clean in the time it takes an older brother to pray. Remember folks, the trick is, his hands never leave the hands he's holding!

Maybe he mumbles 'cause his mouth's full!

But his heart is right.

Sometimes at night, right before they climb into bed, I let the kids pray out loud for whatever requests they may have. Once they found out Mama was going to have a baby (which explained why she was so ill), the pregnancy became the topic of concern.

Joy started out: "Dear Lord, help Mama to feel better real soon and for Betty (one of their baby-sitters) to have her foot feel better quick. Amen."

Jesse went for a more general type prayer. "Dear Lord, help Mama to get better real soon and . . . and . . . and . . . and I would like all people to be safe! Amen."

Jeffrey's prayer caught us a little off guard. His logic was impressive, his concern was heartwarming. "Dear God, please help Mama to start feeling better right away, okay? And, since she is feeling sick, please don't let the baby die. Amen."

Finally, it was John's turn. Uncharacteristically, he didn't mimic his older brothers and sister. A need had arisen in his life which demanded immediate attention. Thus, he took his urgent request to his God in Heaven.

"Dear God . . . please help Daddy change my diaper nicely . . . right now. Amen."

Prayer does change things.

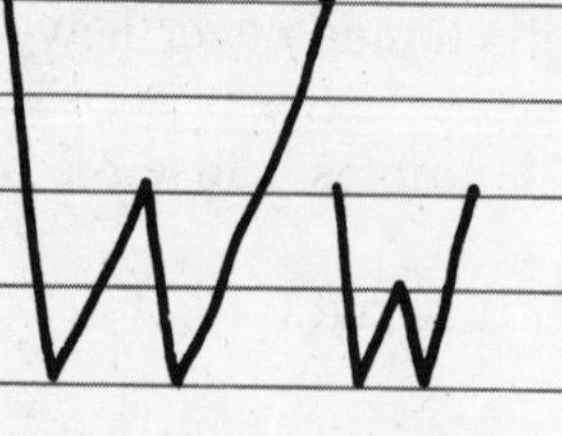

Watch and pray. It's a real education.

Making It Stick

Here's an opportunity for all you excellent parents to take a break. We want to talk about establishing some prayer times with the kids. So if you already pray with your kids, you can stop reading, go make yourself a sandwich, and come back in time to read the rest of the book, okay?

Now for the rest of us who struggle with consistent times of prayer as a family, let's not overlook the obvious. The two scenes described in the above accounts are natural times for talks with the Lord.

Begin praying at mealtimes. Make it more than routine, make it meaningful. Mix it up. You pray or have a child pray, or all pray or even different stuff like praying out loud in unison a Psalm of thanks. Or how about singing a prayer to God? Go around the table and have everyone thank the Lord specifically for the person on their right. (After dinner, pray to the left.)

Don't forget bedtime, either. I find children LOVE to pray right before they go to bed because if they pray, they get to stay up longer. We've had some long prayers at bedtime, but they've been some fine moments of family closeness.

You'll learn a lot from your kids by listening to them pray. You'll discover what's on their minds and what's really important to them.

Also, isn't it encouraging as a parent to realize that your child will drift off to sleep with his mind on the last thing he did that evening . . . talked with God.

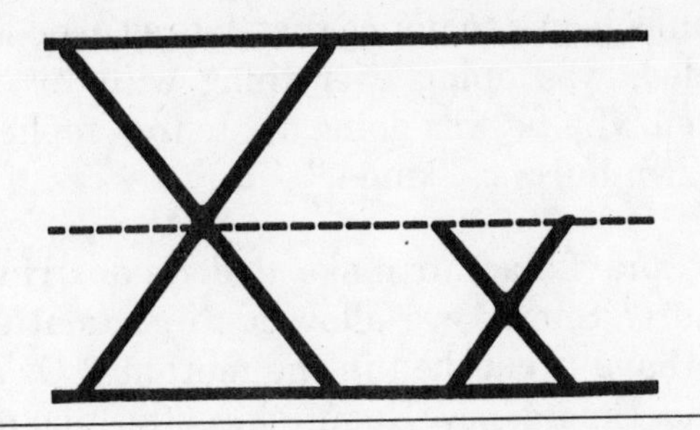

X Rays From God

I have to make a confession. I want this to be a realistic look at family living, so I have to tell the whole truth.

Back under the letter *G* I extolled the virtues of "Gorilla"—i.e., Daddy getting down on the floor and wrestling, while making King Kong sounds. I still believe it's the absolute greatest. My kids would rather play Gorilla than any other game.

But there was this one time when the good stuff backfired.

I was my usual great Gorilla. I was tickling the kids, flipping them over, tossing them around the room, having the best of times when I accidentally sent Jeffrey flying through the air farther than initially intended. He landed in such a way that he hurt his right arm. No blood, no bruises, just the inside kind of hurt.

Well, he cried. I held him. I thought everything was well, when Rhonda began to notice that Jeffrey, who is normally right-handed, was doing everything with his left hand. When asked why he was doing so, Jeffrey replied "'Cause my other arm hurts . . . kinda."

Rhonda and I had to make a decision. How hurt is "kinda" hurt? Should we allow it to go unattended? Or should we have it checked in the morning? Or should we rush to the Emergency Room since the doctor's offices were already closed?

Well, the more we saw that little guy fumble around with his left hand, the more we felt that we should hit the E. R.

Rhonda offered to stay at home with the other three while Jeffrey and I hustled on down to Martin Luther Hospital. We walked into the Emergency Room just in time to observe two or three types of standard sights for these places.

- A youngster hurt in some sort of uniform—obviously an athletic injury.
- A teenager hurt in a motorcycle accident.
- A lady with contractions three minutes apart.

"What are contraptions, Dad?" Jeffrey asked while standing in line.

"It's *contractions*, son, and it means she's going to have her baby real soon."

Well, we finally got to the front of the line. Four forms later we were with a gentle young doctor who wanted to make Jeffrey as comfortable as possible.

"How would you like your own personal banana Popsicle, Jeffrey?" quizzed the doctor with a smile.

Jeffrey's eyes widened and his entire countenance changed as he blurted out an excited, "You bet . . . uh . . . uh . . . please!"

As Jeff licked away, the doctor determined he needed X rays of the arm to be sure all was well. Once in the X-ray room, Jeffrey again looked worried and quite hesitant over the whole process.

"Don't worry," the doctor assured, "this machine is going to look right down inside of you and you won't even feel a thing."

"Oh, like God," was Jeffrey's reply.

The machine did its thing, another Popsicle was dispensed, the X rays came back with no apparent reason for concern, so it was concluded we had a little guy with a bruised arm that would feel better in a few days.

After the entire experience was over, I was in bed thinking through the story and remembered Jeffrey's line about how X rays are like God. The little kiddo was right on.

They are alike.

Aren't you glad God can look right through you? And it doesn't hurt . . . unless of course, He wants it to. He knows my every thought before I think it.

It may sound funny to you, but ten minutes with an X-ray machine caused me to celebrate the greatness of God.

I slipped out of bed, thanked the Lord for who He is, and celebrated His greatness by raiding the freezer and eating a banana Popsicle.

Xx

Xrays can see what's inside. So can God.

Making It Stick

Next time you're sitting around as a family, instead of turning on the television, how about a little game?

Jeffrey was quick to realize the X rays reminded him of God's all-knowing nature. My son is too little to know the term *omniscience*, but he knows what it means. Allow each member of your family to mention a person, place, or thing that reminds them of a quality of God. It could be X rays for omniscience, a wedding picture for God's love, a needlepoint for God's sovereignty, or maybe even a set of training wheels for a bicycle as an example of God's grace!

Remember, this game is for EVERYONE. No one is too young or too old to participate.

End the game when everyone has run out of ideas or at bedtime, whichever comes first.

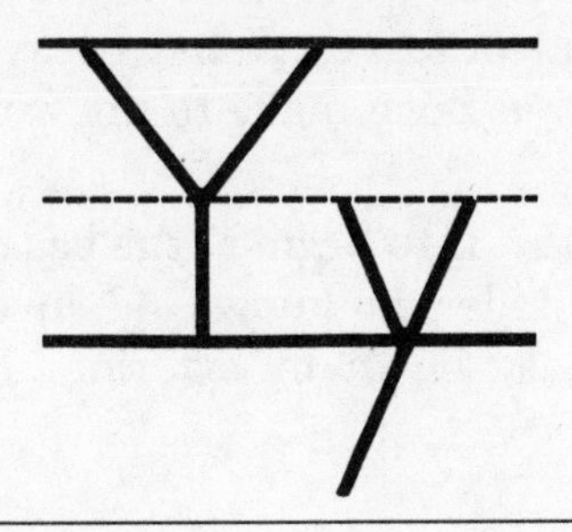

Your Legacy

Ever ask yourself tough questions? The ones without the easy answers. Probing that defies superficial response. Here's one for you to ponder:

When your "three-score and ten" years on this earth are drawn to a close, what will you leave behind as your legacy?

For some it's a business venture of national or even worldwide significance. Others may leave great sums of money to worthwhile causes and charities. Still others may leave a name of fame.

A legacy of this nature isn't bad. In fact, it's quite admirable. But in my mind, there is an even greater legacy that any parent can give to this world . . .

. . . our children.

Let me state it again so it has time to sink in. My children are my greatest legacy. What I leave in them is the richest contribution I can make to my world.

The key to all this is to begin at the basics. I want to pass on to my culture kids who know God, love God, and serve God. That can take on many exteriors, but the inside is unwavering.

What an exciting time it has been for Mama and Daddy to watch our older children come to the place of accepting Jesus Christ as their personal Savior. We anticipate the same thrill with the younger ones.

Interestingly, we don't remember a particular "point" in time when our kids came to Christ. But it has always been an important issue to Rhonda and me, so we've gone over the plan of salvation again and again with our kids. The older ones are old enough to know their need for God to deliver them from their sins, so they asked Jesus to be their Savior the best they knew how. And God did just that. Childlike faith displayed in living examples.

You can't love someone and serve someone until you first know them. So believing in Jesus is their first step in this whole process. I'm so glad they know God.

And they're learning how to love Him and serve Him. Observing my son and daughter breaking out of the mold of childish selfishness by willingly giving of themselves in difficult times and sharing with others when not convenient are both dramatic illustrations of their love for God and His work in their lives. It's refreshing to see them serve God simply as children. They're free from ulterior motives, confusing manipulations, and complicated theologies.

They just love God and want to do good things for Him.

It's important to mention at this point that knowing, loving, and serving God doesn't mean I'm attempting to produce full-time vocational Christian workers. If that happens to occur, fine. If not, fine, too.

I may have a school teacher who knows, loves, and serves God. I may have a policeman who knows, loves, and serves God. Their career choice isn't the issue. It's what's inside that lingers.

The convicting fact about my children being my legacy is that it demands that my life serve as the example of what I want to pass on! After all, I am leaving in them a little bit of me. So in order for them to model their Father, I have to be prepared for them to model their father.

Yy

Years from now they'll re-member you by what they see in your kids.

Making It Stick

What are you doing to insure that your legacy is a good one? Have you given serious consideration to what you will leave behind through the lives of your children?

Let's start at the beginning. Do your children know Jesus Christ as their personal Savior? If so, terrific. If not, what steps can you be taking to provide the right circumstances for each child to personally believe in Christ? It may mean the context of a church with a strong Sunday school program. Or another form of activity with a definite Christian emphasis. Or, it may mean you can have the unforgettable privilege of leading your own child to Christ! If so, remember, make it simple and clear.

We explained over and over to our little ones:

- We all have done wrong things.
- Jesus Christ died on the cross and rose from the dead to pay for all the wrong things we'll ever do.
- If you believe Jesus Christ died on the cross for *you* and receive Him as your personal Savior, He will come to live inside of you and someday you will be with Him in Heaven.

Mom and Dad, it's your privilege and your responsibility. Take it seriously.

When you have assurance that your kids know Christ, you and your mate need to determine what else is important in your legacy. I stated mine in the terms “love God” and “serve God.” You may like those, or you may make your own choice of goals. The critical issue is that you talk it through, unite, and work together in the process of achieving these goals.

Zz

Zipping and Zooming Help Me Zero In

My kids are my best teachers.

But, you know, sometimes it takes a break in the "classroom" to get me to realize anew how remarkable their teaching is.

Yes, it takes some zipping and zooming around to help me zero in on how blessed I am. Some guys zip around in rental cars and zoom around in jets and catch some "ZZZs" in a different hotel room every night as a way of life. I do it as little as possible but it is a *part* of my life.

I can't quite figure out how I feel about being on the road. I love to travel, but I hate to leave home. I hate to be away from home, but it's usually good for my perspective. I guess you call that "mixed feelings."

Being away from home one or two days a month helps

me understand the vital part each member of my family plays in my life. Since I'm writing this while on a three-day trip away from home, let me tell you exactly what I mean.

I miss my daughter, my little Princess, Joy. I miss her contagious laugh, that has never failed to bring a smile to my face, even during tough times.

I even miss the exasperation I feel when she enjoys her newfound freedom using the telephone to call her friends. Believe it or not, I long for that feeling of "taking a number" in order to use the phone because my daughter is chattering away.

I miss Jesse. I miss his corny jokes, his off-key singing, his reciting of television commercials. I want to see his winsome smile, dimples and all.

I even miss being impatient with him. Sometimes he can be so slow to get a job done. I'm thinking maybe I should refer to him as *deliberate* and *purposeful*, rather than slow. I imagine he'd appreciate that change in vocabulary. I miss him stealing meat off my plate when I'm not looking.

I miss Jeffrey. I miss his hugs. I miss the hope and the anticipation he brings to my life. I never know what he'll be wearing, since he's at a stage where he changes clothes seven times a day. I'd love to see those big blue eyes right now. Yes, those eyes that can communicate two hundred different emotions as clear as a bell. And those eyelashes! Any girl would give her all to have those beauties.

I even miss how he begs me to play with him. When I'm home he can get so irritating, but when I'm away all I can think of are those great times we have being together. Don't ever stop bugging me, buddy, or I'll miss out on an entire slice of living.

I miss John. I miss his "I love you, Daddy, you are 'pecial, Daddy," for no reason at all. I miss his kisses. I miss a little guy who can go through Band-Aids faster than any person on earth. I miss his crying 'cause I can't put a Band-Aid on the roof of his mouth.

I even miss his head. The one that's extra hard. The one that bangs into my stomach or face at the most inopportune moments. I miss his forty-four reasons why he can't stay in bed. Yes, I guess I even miss the nights he comes in and sleeps with us.

I miss the Dean of the Faculty—my wife. I miss Rhonda's touch, the light in her eye that says, "Everything is all right," and the chance to hold her hand. I long to talk to her face to face instead of through the courtesy of AT&T. I yearn for our long seasons of silence, where being in the same room together is quite enough. It's called *presence.*

I even miss her "loving" punches in the belly. I miss her probing philosophical questions at night, right before I doze off to sleep.

Yes, I miss them all. Each in their own individual way. They are contributing to a life that without them would be vanilla indeed.

Zipping and zooming around sure does help me zero in on how abundantly God has blessed.

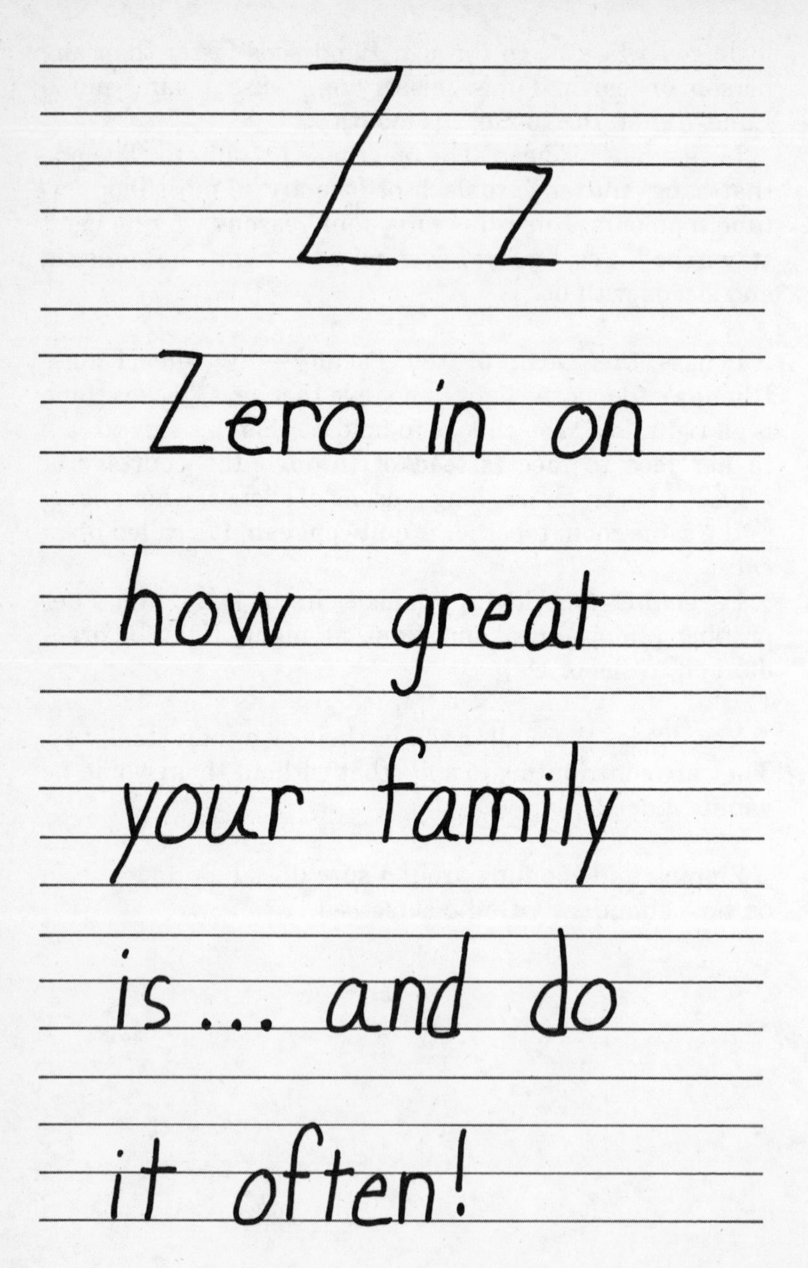
Zz
Zero in on
how great
your family
is... and do
it often!

Making It Stick

Well, I guess we'd call this the bottom line of the entire book. It can all be distilled down to one very important question. Take a moment to ask it of yourself:

Am I allowing my kids to be my best teachers?

Find a blank sheet of paper and write down some of the lessons *you've* learned from your children. Page back over my list of ABCs in order to help spark your thinking. Moms and Dads, those lessons are out there, awaiting your personal discovery.

Conclude your thoughts by talking with God. Thank Him for the blessing of children. Bring each child to remembrance before the Lord. Call each one by name. Review the valuable additions they make to your life.

My kids are my best teachers . . .

. . . it's true for me; is it true for you?